Thomas Merton, Peacemaker

For Larry — With all my Thanks!
Blessings of peace,
John Dear

Meditations on Merton,
Peacemaking,
and the Spiritual Life

Thomas Merton, Peacemaker

Meditations on Merton, Peacemaking, and the Spiritual Life

John Dear

ORBIS BOOKS
Maryknoll, New York 10545

ORBIS BOOKS
Maryknoll, New York 10545

Fathers and Brothers
MARYKNOLL

Founded in 1970, Orbis Books endeavors to publish works that enlighten the mind, nourish the spirit, and challenge the conscience. The publishing arm of the Maryknoll Fathers and Brothers, Orbis seeks to explore the global dimensions of the Christian faith and mission, to invite dialogue with diverse cultures and religious traditions, and to serve the cause of reconciliation and peace. The books published reflect the views of their authors and do not represent the official position of the Maryknoll Society. To learn more about Maryknoll and Orbis Books, please visit our website at www.maryknollsociety.org.

Dear, John, 1959-
    Thomas Merton, peacemaker : meditations on Merton, peacemaking & the spiritual life / John Dear.
        pages cm
    Includes bibliographical references.
    ISBN 978-1-62698-107-2
    1. Merton, Thomas, 1915-1968.   I. Title.
    BX4705.M542D434 2015
    271'.12502—dc23

                                                    2014042335

For Ken Butigan,
Friend and peacemaker

"The God of peace is never glorified by human violence."
—*Thomas Merton*

"There was never anybody else on earth like Thomas Merton. I, for one, have never known a mind more brilliant, more beautiful, more serious, more playful."
—*Mark Van Doren*

"A monk, a man of prayer, a worldly man on the *qui vive*, a recluse for the kingdom's sake, a lucid, cutting mind that in a hundred ways helped us stand somewhere, mainly by standing with us. In entering the monastery, he had taken a large step backward from our world, a tactic the French proverb commends 'in order to leap further.' The leap was not long in coming, a mighty one indeed, a world record."
—*Daniel Berrigan*

"The great Christian is the man or woman who can make me more interested in God than in him or her. A paradoxical tribute, but the highest that can be paid."
—*Archbishop Rowan Williams on Thomas Merton*

"But we have only begun
    to love the earth.
We have only begun
    to imagine the fullness of life.
We have only begun to know
    the power that is in us if we would join
    our solitudes in the communion of struggle."
—*Denise Levertov*

Contents

Introduction

The last hundred years have shown us the worst of systemic evil, with a hundred million dead from warfare, the use of nuclear weapons at Hiroshima and Nagasaki, extreme poverty on an unparalleled level, and the deliberate hastening of catastrophic climate change.

But they have also shown us the best of humanity, with stunning peacemakers of every description from Franz Jägerstätter and Dorothy Day to Mohandas Gandhi and Martin Luther King Jr., to John XXIII and Archbishop Oscar Romero.

In this world of war and despair, these great peacemakers give me hope. They show us a way forward, along the path of nonviolence, toward a new future and the God of peace.

When I was young, I made a conscious decision to study the lives of the great peacemakers, and to meet and befriend the best living peacemakers, in the hope that I might fulfill my vocation to be a peacemaker. I realized I would not learn much about the spiritual life or following Jesus or peacemaking from our presidents, generals, TV newscasters, media pundits, religious officials, or others caught in the trappings of power. So I sought out the great peacemakers of our time, and sat at their feet to hear their lessons of peace—people like Daniel and Philip Berrigan, Bishop Thomas Gumbleton, Mairead Maguire, Mother Teresa, Archbishop Desmond Tutu, Dom Helder Camara, Henri Nouwen, and Thich Nhat Hanh. I also began a lifelong study of the writings of Gandhi, Dr. King, and Dorothy Day.

And from day one, that list included Thomas Merton. I tried to read every book, essay, and letter he wrote. I attended conferences about him, started making regular retreats at the Abbey of Gethsemani, made two retreats in his hermitage, and learned about him from his friends and fellow monks. For over thirty years, as I have traveled the war zones of the world, marched for peace, been arrested and jailed for my protests, and preached the Gospel of peace to the masses, Merton has been my teacher and guide. His writings and example have been a steady, daily source of strength, hope, and light, right up to today.

With gratitude and consolation I think of this peacemaking monk and writer. For while the Berrigans taught me resistance to the culture of war, Dorothy Day models hospitality to the poor, Archbishop Romero demonstrates prophetic truth-telling, and Dr. King exemplifies the methodology of active nonviolence, Thomas Merton embodies for me the creative, spiritual life of peace. By spending hours in prayer, wandering through the woods, reading about every topic under the sun, corresponding with people around the world, and sharing his spiritual discoveries with everyone, Merton lived a full life of peace and shared that peace with the world. There was no violence, no hostility, no meanness in his heart or on his journey; instead, he seemed to discover the freedom of peace within the boundaries of loving, prayerful nonviolence and beheld a vision of peace that saw new horizons few others could see. Because of his soaring intellect, passionate concern for the world, razor-sharp conscience, and ever-deepening faith, he demonstrated a life lived to the full, a life that noncooperates with the forces of death. These days, when life is so cheap, death runs rampant, and few live life to the full, I find his example to be an amazing gift.

January 31, 2015, marks the one hundredth birthday of Thomas Merton. It is a fitting time to take another look at this gospel peacemaker and his wisdom of nonviolence. From the worldly life of his twenties, to his entrance into the Abbey of Gethsemani monastery on December 10, 1941, through twenty-seven years of prayer, community, writing, and teaching, Thomas Merton sought to spend his days with the God of peace. He learned how to live a life of peace and to witness to the good news of peace to the world of war. In doing so, he broke new ground, as one of the first U.S. priests and monks to publicly denounce war, racism, nuclear weapons, and violence. His massive published output changed the conversation, pointing us back toward God and the meaning of our common humanity. Then in 1968, he traveled to Asia in pursuit of what he called "an ontology of nonviolence" in an effort to explore the underlying communion that we already share with every human being. ("Ontology"—one of those unusual philosophical words in metaphysics, refers to "being," "reality," "the ultimate substance," or dare we say, "God.") While attending a monastic conference in Bangkok, he was accidentally electrocuted in a freak accident and died on December 10, 1968, a sudden culmination of his long peacemaking journey. He wanted to plumb the spiritual depths of peace, and he did. His life has borne good fruit for millions, and he still continues to teach us.

Through the writing of this book I have once again looked deeply at the life witness, journal writings, letters, books, and essays of Thomas Merton for insights about how we, too, can become peacemakers in a world of total war. After three decades of journeying with Merton as my teacher and guide, I find several key aspects about Merton's peacemaking life that have shaped my own journey. They may not be that unusual for other students of Merton, but I share them from the perspective of my own peculiar public work in the struggle for justice and peace and in the hope that we can all continue to explore the spiritual life of peace.

"The God of peace is never glorified by human violence," Thomas Merton once wrote. After studying his writings, visiting Gethsemani, and befriending his friends, I came quickly to a conclusion that Merton forgot to mention—that the flip side is also true: "The God of peace is always glorified by human nonviolence."

Merton's nonviolent life glorified the God of peace. He invites us to become people of nonviolence who also glorify the God of peace with our lives, which means we have to renounce violence and set off on our own path of creative nonviolence.

Through my studies of Merton, I've come to believe that the greatest need for the human race right now is a global, spiritual conversion to active nonviolence. What is the point of being devout, religious, and faithful if we still support the culture of war and injustice, corporate greed, nuclear weapons, and environmental destruction? Like Merton, we need to pursue the spiritual depths of nonviolence, to dare follow Jesus all the way to the cross as mature disciples and discover the underlying communion that already exists among us—the truth that we are all sisters and brothers to one another, called to live in peace, love, and nonviolence with each other, with all creatures, and with all creation. As we do, we, too, will break with the culture of war, reach out with an all-inclusive universal love, and begin to live in God's reign of peace here and now.

What does it mean to be a peacemaker? How do we serve the God of peace? How can we move out of the culture of war and violence and step deeper into the spiritual life of nonviolence, into God's reign of peace? How can we become more mature disciples and apostles of gospel nonviolence like Merton? What can we do to help end violence, war, poverty, corporate greed, nuclear weapons, and catastrophic climate change, and create a more nonviolent world? What is the connection between the spiritual life of peace and nonviolence, and the social, economic, and political realities of war and violence? I endeavor to explore these questions with the help of Thomas Merton as teacher and guide.

Peacemaking marks the height and depth and breadth and length of the spiritual life. That, I submit, is one of the core revelations of Thomas Merton's spiritual journey. All of us are on a journey of peace, to the God of peace. We're all learning, like Merton, to make peace with ourselves, with everyone we meet, with all creatures, creation itself, and the Creator. As we become peacemakers, we turn from violence, hatred, fear, and war, and start practicing universal love, boundless compassion, and infinite peace. We see life with new eyes. Our hearts widen to embrace everyone. We are filled with a new spirit of peace. We become, like Merton, people of loving, creative nonviolence.

From now on, we refuse to support the taking of a single life, no matter how noble the cause. We noncooperate with the culture's violence, injustice, and warmaking. We begin to better understand Jesus's life and message, and try to follow him more diligently in our day-to-day lives. We try to cultivate peace within us, that we might radiate peace around us and advance the cause of peace for everyone, everywhere. This is what the spiritual life entails.

Merton invites us to see our lives as a journey in and with and toward the God of peace. As peacemakers, we live and breathe in the Holy Spirit of peace, welcome the risen Christ's resurrection gift of peace, adhere to his Sermon on the Mount teachings on nonviolence, and become not only authentic disciples but sons and daughters of the God of peace. This is a great teaching and one, I suggest, that can enrich our lives, transform the church, and heal our world if we dare take Merton seriously.

Many books have been written about Thomas Merton. I think his embrace of nonviolence and his public work for peace stand at the center of his monastic life. Thus, if we fail to understand his basic foundation in peace and nonviolence, we miss the point of everything he wrote and taught. Merton wants us to become people of contemplative prayer and scripture study so that we might reject violence and war, pursue the gospel way of creative nonviolence and peace, and spend our lives with the God of peace. He wants each one of us to fulfill our spiritual vocations as sons and daughters of the God of peace, brothers and sisters of one another, that we might abolish war once and for all, and build a new world of nonviolence. He's hoping we might carry on his research in the ontology of nonviolence and do our part as public peacemakers to witness to God's reign of peace in our midst.

Merton's teachings can help us discover our true selves, that is, who we already are, and who we are called to be—the sons and daughters of the God of peace. Because this wisdom is still so greatly needed, I offer these reflections on Merton's peace-making lessons in the hope that they will encourage us anew to practice nonviolence, fulfill our own vocations as peacemakers, and welcome Christ's resurrection gift of peace in our hearts and in the world.

Throughout these reflections, I presume the reader is familiar with Thomas Merton's life and writings. I recommend, for newcomers, the biographies *Living with Wisdom* by Jim Forest and *The Seven Mountains of Thomas Merton* by Michael Mott, as well as the seven volumes of Merton's journals and the five volumes of his letters, especially *Thomas Merton on Peace*, edited by William Shannon.

This book is my second on Merton. The first, *The Sound of Listening: A Retreat Journal from Thomas Merton's Hermitage,* based on a month living in Merton's house, is available from Wipf and Stock. This current book was written over a two-year period. The first half was written during a cold winter on my mountaintop hermitage in northern New Mexico in early 2013, and the second half was written during a hot summer in the south of France where I was living in a two-hundred-year-old stone farmhouse with blue shutters called La Petite Solitude, nestled in the old village of La Solitude. Those glorious days in France brought home a forgotten aspect of our protagonist. Merton was born in a gorgeous old village of stone houses with red tile roofs in the south of France. His American parents were artists and moved there so his father could paint, which he did, beautifully, like Cezanne himself. Later Merton went to school in England before settling in New York and finally Kentucky. Deep down, Merton remained French, or at least European, which is one reason for his broad vision, his easy dissent, his love of monasteries, and his pursuit of the quiet, reflective country life. He was raised in a village of peace, nestled in a land torn apart by World War I, and finally found another refuge of peace in the monastery of Gethsemani, and eventually in the woods in a little hermitage.

My reflections are my own musings and meditations based on Merton's life and writings, particularly his teachings on peace and nonviolence. They are not presented systemically; other scholars have written serious analyses of Merton's writings, including his social essays. These reflections, rather, are simple, free-flowing commentaries and gentle meditations on key Merton teachings and moments intended to encourage all those passionate about peace and justice, the contemplative life, the spiritual life, and the long-haul struggle of active nonviolence.

I would like to thank my friends Jonathan Montaldo, Chris Pramuk, and Cynthia and Ken Butigan for proofreading the manuscript and encouraging me to keep at it; Robert Ellsberg of Orbis Books, who said yes to the project before I wrote a word; and all my Merton friends for encouraging me on the journey—Daniel Berrigan, Thich Nhat Hanh, Patrick Hart, Jim Douglass, Jim Forest, Paul Pearson, Joan Baez, Paul Quenon, Richard Rohr, Helen Prejean, Margaret Maggio, Joan Chittister, and Richard Deats; and my Merton friends who have died—

Robert Lax, Tommie O'Callaghan, Myriam Dardenne, Philip Berrigan, John Heidbrink, Robert Giroux, Matthew Kelty, Henri Nouwen, Gordon Zahn, Eileen Egan, and Mary Luke Tobin.

May Thomas Merton the peacemaker help us become better peacemakers and inspire us to pursue a new world without war, injustice, nuclear weapons, or violence—a new world of nonviolence—that we might all welcome God's gift of peace and share that gift with one another.

—John Dear
August 18, 2014
Santa Fe, New Mexico

The Journey to the Desert
with Merton

For me, one of the best places to experience the peace of God is the Benedictine monastery of Christ in the Desert, located in a remote canyon in northern New Mexico.

It's nearly impossible to find. You drive north past Georgia O'Keeffe's house, Bode's General Store, and the Ghost Ranch Presbyterian retreat center. Then, after the majestic Pedernal Mesa, you veer off the highway and travel several miles along a deserted dirt road. You pass endless fields of sagebrush, hemmed in along their perimeters by towering cliffs streaked with red, brown, yellow, and white. At the Rio Chama, you turn right, then proceed at a crawl along the Chama Canyon.

Be patient. It's thirteen miles along a single-lane dirt road. Only then does the road end—right at the monastery, nestled at the foot of a wailing wall of shocking, chiseled red cliffs.

To call it a road is actually to give it too much dignity. It's more of a half-lane dirt path. And it clings to the edge of a cliff some four stories above the river. Getting there is half the fun. The view snatches your breath, but you must resist the temptation to gape in awe. Otherwise, your last act on earth will be to plunge into the river below.

The trek to the monastery is, for me, a good metaphor for the spiritual journey—a dangerous, cliff-hanging journey, full of promise, beauty, and hope.

The remoteness was quite deliberate. Founded in 1964 by

three monks, it remained small and isolated until recent years, when the community welcomed dozens of monks from around the world.

"This is the best monastic building in the country." That's what Thomas Merton wrote on May 17, 1968, when he was searching for a new hermitage away from his monastery, the Abbey of Gethsemani near Bardstown, Kentucky. His abbot, Father Flavian, approved the search. It was one of only a handful of trips Merton ever made outside his monastery before his fateful fall trip to Asia. He flew to San Francisco, visited the Trappistine monastery of the Redwoods in northern California, and then went on to northern New Mexico, recording the experience in a journal, which he edited for publication and titled *Woods, Shore, Desert*. He would stop here again in September on his way to Alaska and then on to Asia. Looking for a more secluded place, he seriously considered the coastline of northern California, a remote village in Alaska, or these canyons in northern New Mexico as a new secret home for himself and a fellow monk or two. Back in New Mexico that September, he met Georgia O'Keeffe for lunch, swam in the Rio Chama, and attended the annual fall dance festival on the Jicarilla Reservation. He found here a place of unparalleled solitude, silence, and peace.

It's still one of the best monastic buildings or spiritual centers in the country, maybe even the world. It's where I go regularly to pray, rest, walk, swim in the Chama, ride horses, and reclaim my inner peace. The landscape never fails to astonish me. The red and yellow cliffs, the cottonwoods, the sagebrush, the stern mountains, the wandering hawks, the bright sun, the pressing silence, and expansive solitude—there's nothing else like it in North America.

"A monastery is not a place where a few retire to deepen their own experience of the meaning of life," Merton wrote during that first visit. "It is also a center where others can come to readjust their perspectives.

"While not blindly rejecting and negating the modern world," he continued, "the monastery nevertheless retains a certain critical distance and perspective which are absolutely necessary as mass society becomes at once more totally organized and more mindlessly violent. In its firm assertion of the basic human values as well as of God's message of salvation, the monastery bears witness to the most fundamental and most permanent truths of life. It remains a sanctuary where both monks and retreatants and others may experience something of that 'peace which the world cannot give.'

"The Monastery of Christ in the Desert," Merton added, "seeks only to keep alive the simplicity of Benedictine monasticism: a communal life of prayer, study, work and praise in the silence of the desert where the Word of God has always been best heard and most faithfully understood."[1]

"The monastery rises at the point where the canyon narrows and the road vanishes into rock and brush," he wrote in his journal. "The monastic church, designed by the Japanese architect George Nakashima, fits perfectly into its setting. Stark, lonely, stately in its simplicity, it gazes out over the sparse irrigated fields into the widening valley. The tower is like a watchman looking for something or someone of whom it does not speak. The architectural masterpiece is a perfect expression, in adobe brick and plaster, of the monastic spirit."[2]

The brown adobe chapel, shaped in the form of a cross, still stands today, rising three stories tall, keeping watch over the canyon. The top two stories are all glass. As you enter through two large carved wooden doors, you see in the center a simple stone altar and on the walls a few bright icons, and above, through the enormous glass window, a looming bank of red cliffs bearing right down on you. It's an overwhelming sight.

On a side wall, and just as moving, is a large Mexican crucifix. It bears all the pathos, dignity, and hope of the world's crucified peoples.

"The monk is one whose gaze is fixed on God," Saint Theodore wrote centuries ago, "who desires God above all else, who applies himself to God, who seeks to serve God alone, in peace with God, and so becomes peace for others."

In that spirit I sit in the silent chapel and take it all in. The silence. The solitude. The beauty. The crucifix. The red cliff. The peace. I begin to breathe again. It's as if I've been holding my breath for months, trying to breathe under water, thrashing to stay afloat in our culture of war. There in that stunning setting of red rock, adobe, and wooden beams, icons, and Mexican crosses, I feel healed, disarmed, refreshed. I remember how to live in peace all over again.

This is precisely why I return to this quiet canyon regularly— so that I may rediscover my own peaceful solitude. This is what Merton our teacher discovered and hopes for all of us.

"If we want to change the world and create peace, we can begin by creating peace within ourselves," the Dalai Lama teaches. "If we practice peace, we can teach the rest of the world." Merton lived out that principle.

Afterward, I walk down along the rushing Rio Chama and sit along its banks. There, sheltered by the cottonwoods, I listen to the rapids. Today the temperature is a stifling ninety-five degrees. What the heck, I think, and jump in, just as Merton did long ago. I take the plunge and meet with polar temperatures. The jolt wakes me, shocks the system, invigorates my senses.

Merton himself was invigorated when he was here. "In our monasticism," he writes in *Woods, Shore, Desert*, "we have been content to find our way to a kind of peace, a simple undisturbed thoughtful life, and this is certainly good, but is it good enough?" This is a crucial question for our times. Yes, we have "a kind of peace," but "is it good enough?" Merton answered:

> I, for one, realize that now I need more. Not simply to be quiet, somewhat productive, to pray, to read, to cultivate leisure. . . . There is a need of effort, deepening, change and transformation. Just to go for walks, live in peace, let change come quietly and invisibly on the inside . . . A return to genuine practice, right effort, need to push on to the great doubt. Need for the Spirit. Hang on to the clear light![3]

As the sun descends I start the treacherous ride back home, to the remote mesa where I live near Galisteo, south of Santa Fe. On the highway at last, I pass rusting, forlorn trailers where there live many of the poorest people in the nation. And I push past Los Alamos, where some of the wealthiest design sinister methods of global destruction at the national nuclear weapons laboratories. The poorest part of the country, the most violent place on earth, and one of the most authentic spiritual centers of North America—all here in the stark New Mexico desert.

By now the prayerful peace of Christ in the Desert has shored my wobbling knees and fortified my deflated spirit. I feel ready to stand again and proclaim the good news of peace to a world of violence and war. In such desert solitude, one meets the risen Christ and receives his resurrection gift of peace. One learns to "live in peace," "let change come quietly," and "hang on to the clear light."

That, for Merton, is the point of monastic life, the spiritual life, gospel peacemaking, indeed our very humanity. It is a lesson he wants to teach all of us.

2

Merton and the Road to Peace

Thomas Merton entered the Trappist monastery to spend his life with "God alone" in prayer and contemplation. Along the way he discovered that prayer and contemplation are not selfish pursuits that make us superior to others. He realized that the life of contemplative prayer renounces all violence and involvement with the culture of war, and pushes us to embrace the whole human race in unconditional love and boundless compassion.

Prayer, meditation, and contemplation lead us to commune with the living God of peace and live in nonviolent communion with all humanity and all creation. Contemplative prayer should widen our hearts to love every human being on earth with the same universal, nonviolent love of God. That global, compassionate love becomes the normal experience of the contemplative peacemaker. It means we are no longer warmakers, no longer supporters of the warmaking culture or the warmaking church. We live in the light of God's peace and are becoming God's peacemakers.

For Merton, contemplative prayer has political consequences. Daily contemplative prayer is an ongoing process of inner disarmament that leads to nonviolent living, which pushed him to be a voice for peace, disarmament, and nonviolence to the whole world. That is what contemplative nonviolence does to any authentic seeker: it disarms us, turns us into peacemakers, and uses us for the global movement of disarmament and nonviolence. This spiritual path can turn our whole lives upside down. It may cause rejection from family, friends, and church leaders along the way, but if we are centered in the God of peace, we will remain peaceful and see ourselves, as if for the first time, following the nonviolent Jesus on the way of the cross, the way of nonviolent resistance to the culture of violence.

Thomas Merton spent about seven hours in prayer every day for twenty-seven years—five or six hours in the monastic liturgy of the hours, morning Mass, and then his own private meditation. But Merton's extraordinary life journey into the monastery, and his astonishing literary output during his monastic life, amaze us not only for his intellectual pursuits but for his spiritual breakthroughs. It's as if he kept on searching, going deeper into the spiritual life in search of truth and God. Like a deep-sea diver or a miner, he made that lonely journey and brought back new discoveries with each effort. Turns out that what he wrote at Christ in the Desert monastery in New Mexico he had been doing all along: "effort, deepening, change, transformation."

As he relates in his best-selling autobiography, *The Seven Storey Mountain*, Merton grew up in France, attended school in England, lived for a while in the Bahamas, lost both his parents, and settled in New York City. He was a brilliant, restless teenager who eventually found his place at Columbia University among some extraordinary teachers, such as Mark Van Doren and Daniel Walsh, and fellow students Bob Lax, Ed Rice, and Robert Giroux. He was a gifted writer and seeker, and that search led him, the proud atheist, to become a Catholic.

It was first in Rome, and then in the churches of New York, that he discovered people sitting in silence, as if they were engaged in some mysterious activity, as if they were attending to some secret presence in those large halls. He wanted to share that mystical experience, even to become a priest, so he followed his heart, was baptized, continued his literary studies and writing, tried his best to become a Franciscan priest, was turned down, and landed a teaching position at St. Bonaventure's in New York. Along the way, he wrote several novels, published poems, and even considered becoming a journalist. At the suggestion of his theology professor Dan Walsh, he went on a religious retreat at the Abbey of Gethsemani Trappist monastery for Holy Week and underwent a profound religious transformation. Six months later, the day after the Japanese attack on Pearl Harbor and the U.S. entrance into World War II, he decided to give everything up, head for the hills, and become a Trappist monk. He took the night train to Kentucky and entered the cloister where he remained for the rest of his life.

But the wise abbot surprised him and urged him, much against his will, to continue to write. So Merton prayed, and unlike the others, he also wrote. He published poetry, the lives of obscure Trappist saints, journals, books on contemplative prayer, a study on apophatic theology, and his widely read autobiography. By the 1950s he was named master of scholastics and later master of novices, and loved this work even as he struggled for greater silence and solitude. His studies continued and widened to include readings on Gandhi, Buddhism, and Russian and Latin American literature. He began to correspond with writers and activists, and then one day in 1958, while standing on a street corner in Louisville, he realized he loved every human being and that his vocation was simply to be a member of the human race. This discovery, one could argue, led to an enormous new burst of writing that addressed every major injustice and systemic evil of the time—from racism, nuclear weapons, and fallout shelters to the Vietnam War, religious bigotry, and empire. It was as if the spiritual journey of prayer and contemplation led him to address the world of violence and war head-on, in ways rarely seen in all of church history up to that time. He pushed open the door for the rest of us, and countless Catholics and other Christians have been addressing the world in all its ugly violence since then.

Like few others, Merton widened the common understanding of the spiritual life to reach out to the whole human race with a universal, compassionate love rooted in nonviolence, which meant that he denounced every form of violence and war that threatened his sisters and brothers anywhere around the world. This vigorous spiritual pursuit took him way beyond the narrow confines of Trappist monasticism, Roman Catholicism, or American patriotism. These breakthroughs led him into a new kind of universal humanity, a oneness with all of creation. In this way, Merton models the spiritual search that keeps on searching, beyond our comforts, fears, and local community, into universal love and global peace. This is the journey that he invites every one of us to undertake.

Around 1960 Merton moved into a hermitage a mile away from the monastery, where he went deeper still into silence and solitude. Even though it was decades before cell phones, iPads, the Internet, or Facebook, Merton touched people around the world through his correspondence—over ten thousand letters alone (housed at the Merton Center in Louisville, Kentucky) to correspondents around the globe. After the election of a new abbot in 1967 Merton was allowed to travel, so he accepted an invitation to a monastic conference in Asia. He journeyed through India and Sri Lanka, met with the Dalai Lama, gave a series of talks, and eventually landed in Bangkok to address an international gathering of monastic leaders. After his talk on the morning of December 10, 1968, he returned to his room; took a shower; bumped into an old, upright electric fan; and was accidentally electrocuted. He was fifty-three years old.

Reflecting on his life and teachings nearly fifty years after his death, one hundred years after his birth, we can see the global impact his life has had upon the church and the world. "For the next two hundred years," theologian David Tracy Ellis wrote recently, "we will all be trying to catch up to Merton." I think it is well worth our time and energy to ponder his journey and writings that we too might go deeper into the life of God and bring forth new fruit for peace.

Merton sought the God of peace year after year, through trial and error, success and failure, brokenness and wholeness. That is one of his first lessons for us—the example of the contemplative life as an ever unfolding journey into the God of love and peace that accepts all the social, economic, and political consequences of nonviolence. As we strive for the God of love and peace, we stretch and grow and break and open up to embrace the whole human race and creation itself. This difficult path of wisdom, Merton demonstrates, leads to universal love, compassion, peace, and nonviolence. It may not be the outcome most Christians want, for in a world of violence and war, it will lead to rejection and the cross, but that's precisely where the mature, faithful disciple is headed—to the crucified, risen Christ and his kingdom of peace, love, and nonviolence.

The young, enthusiastic Merton wrote a beloved best seller, some beautiful poems, and moving meditations on the spiritual life. The older, wiser, more mature Merton is dangerous. He takes on every political issue; criticizes the nation, the church, and the monastery; and steps into the messy consequences of the cross. He no longer fits into mainstream American Christianity. He does not make us feel good. He's more like a disturber of the peace than a feel-good peacemaker, and he suffered for his stand. In that sense, he steps into the prophetic tradition and shows us what an authentic discipleship to the nonviolent Jesus might look like today.

Merton challenges us to our own authentic spiritual search, to keep at it and not give up, to seek the God of peace with the same radical openness, even into the fullness of nonviolence with all its political consequences, even unto the cross. That means living a life of contemplative prayer, welcoming God's gift of peace every day, and becoming a new breed of Christian—men and women of gospel nonviolence.

3

Contemplative Nonviolence, Not Contemplative Violence

Daniel Berrigan once told me the story of speaking in 1965 to a packed church of cloistered Carmelite nuns. He had been invited to read his latest poems. As he read his poetry he began to reflect on the growing U.S. war in Vietnam and urged the sisters to pray for peace and speak out against U.S. warmaking.

Almost as one, the congregation exploded. How dare you attack our country? they shouted. If we don't kill those communists, they'll invade us and take over! they said. Kill them all, the nuns agreed.

Dan was shocked. Here were "holy" contemplative women who spent many hours a day in prayer and liturgy advocating our country's murder of children in another land. *How could this be?* he thought. How is it that contemplative people can support war and violence? Why do we so easily compartmentalize our private spiritual life, even our religious, communal life, from our public life in the world? Shouldn't these contemplatives be the first to see the children of Vietnam as our sisters and brothers, and to advocate for them?

Dan Berrigan's experience should haunt every peacemaker and anyone who cares about the spiritual life and a future of peace. How can we help people everywhere, including decent people of faith and prayer, to break from the culture of war and injustice and embrace God's reign of peace completely, even with all the publicly distressing social, economic, and political implications?

Over the course of thirty years of public peacemaking, I've seen that disconnect nearly every day. Few Christians in the United States understand Jesus's nonviolence and how, I would submit, it is normative for our own lives. So many ordinary Christians, so many priests, ministers, nuns, and bishops whom I have met—good, decent people who spend quality time each day in prayer and scripture study—still support war, bombing raids, drone attacks, U.S. nationalism, and nuclear weapons. They were never taught the spirituality and boundaries of Jesus's nonviolence. At some point, they stopped their spiritual search because its political implications were too demanding, threatening, and life-changing. They let a false spirituality of violence and war corrupt their vision, and they refuse to see clearly with the eyes of Christ's peace a new vision of the world at peace.

I remember, for example, making a retreat at a cloistered monastery on the West Coast. By chance I met the former abbot, and we struck up a friendly conversation about the monastery and the church. He knew of my work for peace, and how I had coauthored the Pax Christi Vow of Nonviolence, which ten thousand people professed in the 1980s as a way to formalize their commitment to peace. He proudly told me that in January 1991, just as the U.S. military began its war on Iraq, he and three other monks had professed that vow. I was happy to hear his story, but after a moment I paused and wondered out loud: Only four monks professed the vow of nonviolence? What about the rest of the community, the other thirty monks? He put his head down. "The rest of them were all in favor of the war," he said sadly. "They are die-hard, patriotic Americans, and totally supported the killing of Iraqis."

Thomas Merton and other legendary peacemakers such as Dorothy Day, Martin Luther King Jr., and Daniel Berrigan insist that the Christian life, the spiritual life, and church life require a complete rejection of violence and war and a complete acceptance of Jesus's gift of peace. Jesus was perfectly nonviolent, they insist. He blessed peacemakers and commanded us to put down the sword and love even our enemies. There's no talk in the Gospels of justified warfare, deterrence, collateral damage, an acceptable number of casualties, or support for empire. Jesus upholds a vision of nonviolence—the reign of God—and calls us to welcome it, enter it, live in it now. Merton tried to do that and, in doing so, opened up a new spirituality of peace and nonviolence that remains crucially needed today.

Merton concluded that the life of prayer, spirituality, contemplation, mysticism, and search for God excludes violence, rejects warfare, and pursues an active universal love for every human being on the planet. The spiritual life, Merton knew, makes us all peacemakers. The life of prayer leads us to the God of peace, who disarms us and sends us forth into the world of war as God's disarming agents of peace. These connections, Merton and his friend Father Daniel Berrigan believed, need to be made now more than ever, as we stand on the brink of global destruction and catastrophic climate change.

Merton reclaimed the long Christian tradition of prayer, meditation, and contemplation and made it accessible to hundreds of millions of people. He demonstrated through his life and writings that every one of us can be a contemplative. Prayer, meditation, even silence and solitude show us ourselves, lead us to God, and bear the good fruit of peace for ourselves and humanity, he taught.

But Merton insisted that the life of prayer, meditation, contemplation, and spirituality means that we reject war and violence in all its forms, once and for always, and that, from now on, we are people of nonviolence, called to be nonviolent peacemakers.

Prayer and contemplation are useless if they make us more violent, more supportive of war, more trusting in nuclear weapons for our national security, Merton taught. Indeed, any prayer that fans the flames of violence and war cannot be authentic. All prayer, meditation, and contemplation begin and end within the framework of nonviolence. To turn to God in prayer is to turn to a higher power of peace, to be disarmed and transformed into a disarming presence in the world. Contemplative prayer helps us see beyond the lies of the culture of war to recognize every human being on the planet as our sisters and brothers and to deepen that communion of peace that the God of peace gave to us long ago. Contemplatives, therefore, are by their very nature peacemakers, not warmakers.

Contemplative prayer, as Thomas Merton taught it, is a daily practice that opens us to the God of peace. It is a lifelong spiritual journey on a path of peace. It leads us out of the culture of violence and war into God's peaceful presence, to the point that our broken hearts become disarmed and we start to practice the very nonviolence of Jesus and radiate his own personal peace. Merton's contemplative prayer invites us to put down the sword, get rid of our guns, stop hurting others, renounce support for war, quit the military and militaristic solutions, and pursue a new vision of unity with the human family and all creation. Once we step into the boundaries of nonviolence, then the journey of contemplative prayer can take off. Perhaps for the first time, we realize we cannot rely on violence, weapons, or other idols for our security, but that all our security comes from God alone. But over time, our experience of God's unconditional, disarming love in the daily encounter of contemplative prayer lessens our fear and increases our faith and trust in God.

For Merton, the spiritual life was a journey of peace along the way of gospel nonviolence to the God of peace. He invited us to pray and contemplate God daily, that we also might discover the presence of the God of peace as he had in the monastery. He was not calling us to an unrealistic, sugar-coated life in la-la land—far from it. His understanding of prayer is so mature that it means dealing with the roots of violence within us every day as we come before the God of peace in all our brokenness and darkness. Not only do we face our inner violence and let God heal us, we face the world's violence and cooperate with God's healing of humanity and the world.

Having gleaned all this from Merton's life and writings, I hear Merton invite us to practice what I call *contemplative nonviolence*. He wants us to enter into the presence of the God of peace, wait upon the God of peace, and do whatever the God of peace wills for us individually and collectively. But if Merton calls us to be people of contemplative nonviolence, that's because he knows that we are people of violence, even contemplative violence. Many of us spend our lives saying rote prayers that are focused ultimately on ourselves and not the living God ("Help me win the lottery!"). We do all the talking, make selfish demands of God, ignore God's love for us, and turn away from God's call to love everyone with a universal, non-violent love. In this spirituality of violence, we say our prayers but ignore the violence within us. So we go on supporting the culture of war, upholding our nation, and turning our backs on the poor—all while thinking we are especially holy people. Meanwhile, we do not know God, ourselves, or the millions of sisters and brothers around the world who suffer and die due to our systemic injustice.

Contemplative nonviolence calls for an entirely different approach. Instead of doing the talking, we do all the listening. Instead of making demands on God, God makes demands upon us. Through contemplative nonviolence, we focus on the nonviolent Jesus and the Holy Spirit of peace, love, and compassion, and in so doing, we undergo a lifelong, daily, ongoing conversion to nonviolence, a new beginning that starts every time we sit to meditate. In this contemplative practice, we deal with our inner violence and surrender ourselves to the God of peace, even if we do not want to or do not understand why we should. We undergo a cold-turkey withdrawal from violence, much like a drug addict getting off heroin. It's painful and uncomfortable—and literally our salvation. This journey for the sobriety of nonviolence will continue for the rest of our lives.

In contemplative violence, oddly enough, we can be quite peaceful with ourselves—as we go forward in our unconscious support of war and empire. Merton wrote a biting essay about Adolf Eichmann as the best modern example of this devout insanity—which appeared to many Germans as the ultimate sanity. A nonviolent person often does not feel centered or peaceful, because he or she is attending to an inner violence as well as the world's violence. It's a long-haul, ever-deepening awareness, a daily surrender of our violence to God, so that over time we are transformed by God's disarming love and sent into the world of war as God's peacemakers. Merton underwent and taught about this journey, a journey that few really want, yet that God requires of us all.

Merton urges us to take quality time every single day in the presence of God. For Merton, that means entering the absence of God. For decades, Merton advocated the apophatic way of darkness, where we sit in what he called "the Void" with no thoughts, no words, no feelings, no images, and no holy references. If God chooses at God's leisure to show up, great. If not, we remain in the darkness of peace and wait in peace for God. This form of contemplative prayer allows the peace of God to slowly overtake us. We die to ourselves and all that the culture of war could offer, surrendering into the abyss of God. In the presence/absence of the God of peace, we are disarmed, literally and figuratively. This inner disarmament cannot be measured, but it happens, slowly, over a lifetime of daily contemplation. In that prayer, we occasionally feel the infinite love of God and are stirred to love ourselves and others, even our enemies, with that same unconditional, universal nonviolent love. We give God our inner violence and resentments, our hurts and anger, our pain and wounds, our bitterness and vengeance. We grant clemency and forgiveness toward those who have hurt us, and move from anger, revenge, and violence to compassion, mercy, and nonviolence. This quiet, daily, uneventful experience of contemplative prayer transforms us into peacemakers. Though it might feel like sitting in darkness, it enables us to walk in light.

My experience of contemplative prayer comes from Ignatian spirituality, which differs from monastic or apophatic spirituality. Saint Ignatius encourages the use of one's imagination in prayer. He invites us to imagine sitting with the nonviolent Jesus, speaking to him, listening to him, feeling his peaceful presence, allowing ourselves to be disarmed and healed, and getting ready to face the world in his spirit of love and peace. But while Ignatian spirituality offers a different approach, it, too, is a form of contemplative nonviolence that sends us forth as peacemakers into the world of war.

If we make contemplative nonviolence our daily practice, over years and decades we will begin like Merton and the saints to radiate personally the peace we seek politically, and to advocate publicly for universal peace. We, too, will stand up publicly and speak against war and witness for peace with a new kind of authority, based in the Word of God and the presence of the God of peace, which is what the God of peace calls all of us to do.

4

The Fruit of an Inner Unity
Already Realized

———————

The contemplative work of inner conversion, inner disarmament, and inner peacemaking as the key to peace for the world held Merton's interest throughout his life. It's what he admired most about Mahatma Gandhi, and what he tried to achieve for himself. Merton wrote about Gandhi as a high school student in England and spent a good portion of the late 1950s studying in detail Gandhi's writings on nonviolence. As Merton became involved with peace movement leaders in the early 1960s, he assembled a collection of Gandhi's writings, *Gandhi on Nonviolence*, which became a strong encouragement for those struggling for civil rights, nuclear disarmament, and an end to the Vietnam War.

Merton's long introductory essay remains one of the most insightful examinations of the spiritual basis of Gandhi's life and work. Merton observed that Gandhi's political revolution sprang from an inner, spiritual revolution of the heart. "Gandhi's nonviolence was not simply a political tactic which was supremely useful and efficacious in liberating his people," Merton wrote. "On the contrary, [his] spirit of nonviolence sprang from an inner realization of spiritual unity in himself. The whole Gandhian concept of nonviolent action and *satyagraha* is incomprehensible if it is thought to be a means of achieving unity rather than as the fruit of inner unity already achieved."[1]

This is a powerful insight about the nature of the spiritual life and its social, economic, political, and even global implications. While Gandhi remains perhaps the greatest activist, peacemaker, and leader of recent centuries, his public work sprang from the disciplined inner disarmament of his heart and the inner cultivation of peace, freedom, and nonviolence. Merton taught that if we wish to advance the cause of peace and disarmament, peace and disarmament must take root first within ourselves; we must diligently do our inner work, and then it will spread far and wide in the Spirit of God. Gandhi and Merton together taught that the more we cultivate interior nonviolence and interior disarmament, the more nonviolence and disarmament will spread throughout the world, for we will model that spirit and thus be channels of it. Our very presence will disarm others, but the deeper we go interiorly, the greater we can disarm even nations and empires.

Interestingly, Gandhi's contemplative nonviolence and community-based peacemaking began after a visit to a Trappist monastery near Durban, South Africa, in the late 1890s. Gandhi set up his own monastic community called Phoenix Settlement, and then a second ashram called Tolstoy Farm. As he and his coworkers struggled against systemic racism and injustice in South Africa, they shared manual labor and all possessions, and prayed together every day. Gandhi spent two hours each day in prayer for over forty-five years, and in the last years of his life, he took Mondays as a weekly day of silence. The witness of his local Trappist monastery helped him become the great spiritual and political peacemaker we know.

Merton saw this spiritual practice as the foundation of Gandhi's active nonviolence. Merton wanted all those who care for justice and peace to live a similarly disciplined, contemplative practice so that our inner disarmament might deepen and our inner peace might bear the good fruit in the disarmament of the world. Merton was making connections from Gandhi's life that few others had, and trying to live them in his own monastic routine. This spiritual discovery remains true today and can be attempted by anyone willing to engage in that inner work of disarmament for the pursuit of a nonviolent heart that can be a disarming presence in our warring world.

In that light, Merton agreed with Gandhi that nonviolence

is the only hope for humanity's future. "Nonviolence requires a supernatural courage only obtainable by prayer and spiritual discipline," Merton wrote. "This courage demands nothing short of the ability to face death with complete fearlessness and to suffer without retaliation. Such a program is meaningless and impossible, Gandhi thinks, without belief in God."[2] Merton continued,

> Nonviolence is for Gandhi the basic law of our being. That is why it can be used as the most effective principle for social action, since it is in deep accord with the truth of humanity's nature and corresponds to humanity's innate desire for peace, justice, order, freedom and personal dignity. Since violence degrades and corrupts humanity, to meet force with force and hatred with hatred only increases humanity's progressive degeneration. Nonviolence, on the contrary, heals and restores humanity's nature, while giving humanity a means to restore social order and justice. Nonviolence is not a policy for the seizure of power. It is a way of transforming relationships so as to bring about a peaceful transfer of power, effected freely and without compulsion by all concerned, because all have come to recognize it as right. Since nonviolence is in humanity's nature itself, it can be learned by all. . . . All should be willing to engage in the risk and wager of nonviolence because violent policies have not only proved bankrupt but threaten humanity with extinction.[3]

Violent policies threaten humanity with extinction. In a world with over thirty wars, billions suffering in extreme poverty, thousands of nuclear weapons at the ready, and catastrophic climate change bearing down upon us, Gandhi—and Merton—are both being proved right. Violence has failed us, and our acceptance of the structures and systems of violence is destroying the very planet and all its creatures. We all have to renounce our violence and take up the journey of nonviolence, and work for the disarmament and healing of humanity and the world. But Merton urges us to go even further—to plumb the depths of nonviolence within, to undergo such a conversion of heart that we become spiritually explosive, disarming, healing people who bear the good fruit of peace for many.

For a cloistered monk and reclusive hermit, Merton's impact on the world is astonishing and proves his point. Any one of us can be a force for truth, healing, disarming love, and justice—if we give it our full effort and attention, indeed, if we surrender our lives to this way of God. For Merton then, peace and non-violence are about God. They are the way to God, the way with God, and God's very spirit. Once Merton realized this insight through his study of Gandhi and Buddhism, and his encounters with peace movement leaders, he sought to explain the way of nonviolence to the church and the world. His profound insights can still help us if we dare take them to heart.

"The kingdom of God *is* nonviolence," Gandhi once wrote. Merton saw, as few others did, that for Gandhi the struggle of active nonviolence was nothing less than the struggle for the reign of God. "When the practice of nonviolence becomes universal," Gandhi concluded, "God will reign on earth as God does in heaven." That statement sums up the spiritual journey, the political task ahead of us.

Throughout our daily lives we practice nonviolence and teach it far and wide so that God reigns in our hearts and on earth as God reigns in heaven. Merton tried to embody that teaching, to unleash the contemplative power of nonviolence within his heart that God's reign of peace might spread further and further. He inspires me to undertake that same spiritual/political journey.

It's a calling every one of us should accept.

5

Nonviolence Depends Entirely on God and God's Word

Thomas Merton was not just a great teacher. First of all, he was a great student. He was a lifelong student of spirituality, prayer, theology, peace, justice, poetry, history, culture, language, architecture, nature, politics, and all things human and divine. He was constantly studying, reading, learning, writing, and searching for the truth. His serious study of Gandhi and Buddhism in the 1950s prepared him for the political tumult of the 1960s. He had something useful to offer those on the front lines. By the time he met people like Father Daniel Berrigan, A. J. Muste, and peace movement leaders from the Fellowship of Reconciliation and the Catholic Worker, he had become both a student and teacher of gospel nonviolence.

I think that's what each one of us has to do. Sooner or later, given these cataclysmic times, anyone serious about the spiritual life has to become a student of gospel nonviolence and a public teacher of gospel nonviolence.

Merton's journals from the early 1960s bear out his transformation and public commitment, as he comes to grips with his inner violence and personal behavior and decides to address the most serious issues threatening the church and humanity. "Some professor of nonviolence I am," he writes in his journal after one bad day in the early 1960s. He saw himself as a student and a teacher of nonviolence, which is a helpful—and manageable—goal for all of us. All of us can be lifelong students of peace and nonviolence, and all of us can teach peace and nonviolence.

What did Merton learn and teach? First of all, the futility of violence and war. He was coming to the conclusion that war is obsolete, that war never brings peace, that war can now kill millions of innocent civilians, and that war could lead to total destruction. Second, that nuclear weapons, in particular, are unchristian, immoral, idolatrous, illegal, and downright impractical, if not outright suicidal. No follower of the nonviolent Jesus can ever support nuclear weapons. Indeed, every Christian needs to speak out against them and work for their abolition, if we are ever to rid ourselves of this evil. Third, that violence and war are not of God, that God is a God of peace, that the spiritual life is a life of peace, that we are called to live in peace. Fourth, that the life of peace requires the practice of nonviolence within ourselves, among ourselves, and for all society and international relations. Merton lamented the history of violence within the church and spoke out against the scandal of church leaders who blessed our wars and weapons. He knew such behavior was heretical, blasphemous, and idolatrous, and he grieved it, prayed over it, and wrote against it.

Merton did not live to read the thousands of new scripture commentaries published over the last few decades. He was beginning to understand the nonviolence of Jesus, but without the benefit of brilliant studies that have since unpacked the depths of Jesus's nonviolence—how Jesus formed disciples to be nonviolent peacemakers, how his proclamation of God's reign invoked a new world of peace, how he engaged the empire through nonviolent resistance, and how he underwent execution in perfect nonviolence to reveal the love of God and the peace of resurrection. We have many more resources to understand the depths and practicality of Jesus's teachings in the Gospels than Merton ever had, yet Merton knew instinctively that Christianity required peacemaking, so he stood up publicly and began to teach the Christian message of peace. As one of the most famous Catholics in the world, it was a bold move, one that provoked the ire of church authorities and ordinary churchgoers, but Merton knew that this central truth needed to be taught, and that if he wanted others to teach nonviolence, he had to do it as well.

But Merton went further than most teachers of nonviolence.

Bringing the full weight of monasticism, the history of mysticism, and his own spiritual journey to the vision of nonviolence, Merton understood that God was nonviolent and that a nonviolent life required a living faith in the God of peace and nonviolence. For Merton, the living God was not a god of war, but a God of peace—infinite peace for one and all and for eternity. Merton knew that most Christians around the world worshipped a false god who blessed their wars and used violence against us. He pointed us toward a living God of peace who renounced violence but gave us the freedom to choose violence or nonviolence. Adherence to the false gods of war and weapons was just plain old-fashioned idolatry, which Merton took seriously as the first prohibition among the Ten Commandments and the greatest of all sins.

Over the years Merton changed basic Catholic and Christian theology and spirituality. He was inadvertently developing a theology and spirituality of peace that rejected violence and war, and pursued a new kind of humanity and world. More, he turned us back toward a God of peace that we are called to serve and glorify with our lives.

"The chief difference between violence and nonviolence," Merton wrote in his brilliant essay "Blessed Are the Meek: The Christian Roots of Nonviolence," "is that violence depends entirely on its own calculations. Nonviolence depends entirely on God and God's word."[1] This profound insight deserves our serious consideration and personal practice.

Violence comes from the void of chaos and always leads to further chaos and death. Nonviolence flows from the God of peace, the Christ of peace, and the Holy Spirit of peace. Nonviolence is the way of God. To practice nonviolence here on earth means trusting in the God of peace and nonviolence every day of our lives. As people of nonviolence who rely solely on God for our safety and security, we believe, we pray, we trust, and we persevere. That is why we pray, why we believe, why we trust, why we persevere. We need God! We do not place our trust in guns or weapons of war. We do not own or operate guns or weapons. We do not place our trust in nations or their armies. We do not resort to violent self-defense. We place our trust completely in the God of peace. Those who depend on violence and weapons for their security do not need God; those who live an unarmed life need God for their safety and security.

God alone can help us survive the culture of violence and war. We depend on God—personally, communally, nationally, globally. As we grow in faith, we realize that every day is a gift from the God of peace, that our survival depends on God, and lo and behold, our survival is already guaranteed. In this light, with this kind of simple faith, one can understand why Merton would spend seven hours every day in prayer and communal worship, and why we too can spend more time each day with God, trusting in God, living with God.

More, we learn with Merton that living a life of nonviolence means living our lives according to the Word of God. That holy word is quite specific. Merton has in mind the teachings of nonviolence in the Sermon on the Mount and the four Gospels. There we hear clear commandments: "You have heard it said, 'Thou shalt not kill'; but I say to you, do not even get angry with one another. Be reconciled. Offer no violent resistance to one who does evil. Put down the sword. Do unto others as you would have them do unto you. Love your enemies that you may be sons and daughters of your heavenly God who lets his sun rise on the good and the bad and lets the rain fall on the just and the unjust." These and other teachings delineate a specific path, a daily renunciation of violence, the daily practice of nonviolence, and the steady cultivation of a spirit of love, compassion, and peace.

As contemplatives of peace and nonviolence, we base our lives on the Word of God. That's what Merton's daily life shows us. Like Gandhi and Merton, we, too, should read from the Gospels and the Sermon on the Mount daily, for the rest of our lives, and try to regulate our lives according to these teachings. They should become the focus of our energy, our time, our conversation, our work, and our worship. We adhere to Jesus's commandments of peace, love, and nonviolence, even if we do not yet fully understand them. We pray as if our very lives depend on the God of peace—as in fact they do. The more we do so, the more we realize the utter waste of weapons, war, and fear itself. The more we do, the more we discover new blessings of peace in our own lives. Along the way, we become not just students and teachers of peace but apostles and prophets of the God of peace.

6

The One Task That God Has Imposed on Us

"The question of peace is so important that I do not believe anyone who takes his Christian faith seriously can afford to neglect it," Merton wrote to his friend Etta Gullick in the early 1960s.

> I do not mean to say that you have to swim out to nuclear submarines carrying a banner, but it is absolutely necessary to take a serious and articulate stand on the question of nuclear war. And I mean against nuclear war. The passivity, the apparent indifference, the incoherence of so many Christians on this issue, and worse still, the active belligerency of some religious spokesmen, especially in this country, is rapidly becoming one of the most frightful scandals in the history of Christendom. I do not mean these words to be in any sense a hyperbole. The issue is very grave.[1]

Merton's early warning against war and weapons of mass destruction sounded such an alarm in my mind that I did indeed undertake many bold actions for disarmament—even swimming out toward a Trident submarine and undergoing arrest for disrupting the business of nuclear war preparations. Sometimes I wish more people would come forward with similar outrageous acts of nonviolence to wake people up, but needless to say, Merton's letter, like a thousand others, points to the most frightful scandal in the history of Christianity, which continues to this day.

These are the over-riding concerns of Merton's lifelong prayer and spiritual quest. In his twenties, he was a conscientious objector to World War II. Before Pearl Harbor he in effect renounced the military and entered a Trappist monastery. There he spent many hours a day in prayer and study, year after year, writing and pondering every angle of the spiritual life, so that by the 1960s, as an elder in the Order and one of the world's most recognized spiritual teachers, he announced that the most important task before us is the abolition of war, nuclear weapons, and violence itself. If we took him seriously, and believed the conclusion of his spiritual journey, we would join every effort to end war, dismantle our nuclear arsenal, and promote nonviolent conflict resolutions to all global conflicts.

Merton had studied the rise of Nazi Germany, World War II, and the U.S. atomic bombings of Hiroshima and Nagasaki. He let the realities of nuclear weapons and global violence enter his daily meditation before the God of peace. He saw how deadly our capacity for violence had become, and he realized that he had to do something about it, even though he was just a priest, a monk, and a writer. He prayed about it, talked about it, and wrote about it, and in doing so he challenged the church, the nation, and the world to wake up, grow up, and pursue a new culture of peace.

"I don't feel that I can in conscience, at a time like this, go on writing just about things like meditation, though that has its point," he wrote to Dorothy Day on August 23, 1961. "I cannot just bury my head in a lot of rather tiny and secondary monastic studies either. I think I have to face the big issues, the life and death issues, and this is what everyone is afraid of."[2]

He sat down and wrote a passionate new book on the subject—*Peace in the Post-Christian Era,* which his superiors quickly banned. "Never was opposition to war more urgent and more necessary than now," he declared in it. "Never was religious protest so badly needed." His fearful Trappist superiors were appalled. Their response only proved to Merton the seriousness of the crisis. So Merton turned to smaller publications and started privately mimeographing his writings (most notably, "The Cold

War Letters") as well—anything to get out the message of peace.

Perhaps his most famous statement was one of his earliest, a lead article for the *Catholic Worker* called "The Root of War Is Fear." There, Merton threw down the gauntlet and challenged every Christian to rise to the occasion and fulfill the gospel mission of peace:

> The duty of the Christian in this time of crisis is to strive with all our power and intelligence, with our faith and hope in Christ, and love for God and humanity, to do the one task which God has imposed upon us in the world today. That task is to work for the total abolition of war.

~

> There can be no question that unless war is abolished the world will remain constantly in a state of madness and desperation in which, because of the immense destructive power of modern weapons, the danger of catastrophe will be imminent and probable at every moment everywhere.

~

> The church must lead the way on the road to the non-violent settlement of difficulties and toward the gradual abolition of war as the way of settling international or civil disputes. Christians must become active in every possible way, mobilizing all their resources for the fight against war.

~

> Peace is to be preached and nonviolence is to be explained as a practical method. Prayer and sacrifice must be used as the most effective spiritual weapons in the war against war and like all weapons, they must be used with deliberate aim: not just with a vague aspiration for peace and security, but against violence and war. This implies that we are also willing to sacrifice and restrain our own instinct

for violence and aggressiveness in our relations with other people. We may never succeed in this campaign but whether we succeed or not, the duty is evident.[3]

This essay is one of the most important teachings of our times. Merton dares to proclaim that the number-one task imposed upon us all by God is "to work for the total abolition of war." Further, he insists that the church must lead the way in nonviolence for the abolition of war. Then he teaches that Christians must become *active*, that is, they must be personally involved in some particular struggle for disarmament and justice. Finally, he concludes with the insight that whether we succeed is ultimately not in our hands: the important point is to do our duty, to do what we can, to do our part in abolishing war.

Who takes this Merton declaration seriously? Far too few. I believe this prophetic declaration is as true today as the day it was written over fifty years ago. Each one of us has to get involved in the struggle to abolish war, with all the difficulty, frustration, and futility that that entails.

In effect, Merton the monk and hermit summons us to become peace activists, to join the global grassroots movement for disarmament, justice, nonviolence, and peace. This is the natural outcome of the life of prayer, he announces. The spiritual journey leads us to enter the world's violence in a spirit of prayerful nonviolence and work for peace and disarmament. I think Merton could say this because, actually, he had become a peace activist. Merton was *active* in ways that few are. He wrote to thousands of people, regularly churned out powerful books, published a wide range of essays, met all kinds of people, and tried to bring his own community up to speed about the issues of the day.

Daniel Berrigan told me long ago that few people have ever understood his best friend, Thomas Merton. Merton cared passionately for peace, nonviolence, and disarmament, he insisted, and because few share that passion, they can't quite understand him. Author and activist Jim Douglass writes that his friend Merton, alone in his hermitage in the woods, did more for peace than most activists. Merton read far more and understood the details of the Vietnam War, nuclear weapons, racism, poverty, and the imperial ambitions of America than most, and he connected those horrors with the questions and crises of faith and violence in the United States and the world. He used his talents to strengthen the peace movement and change the church. He did what he could, which was an enormous contribution to the movement, the church, and the world.

Since Merton wrote his declaration in "The Root of War Is Fear," the world's addiction to war has only increased. Some argue that we now live in a world of permanent warfare that is as dangerous as the days of the Cuban missile crisis. If Merton is correct, then this task "imposed upon us by God" remains imposed upon us. This is still the will of God, the number-one desire of God—that we abolish war once and for all, and learn to live in peace and nonviolence with one another. The spiritual life and the life of the church must include some work for the abolition of war, if it wants to do God's will. Get busy with the task at hand, Merton writes. God is waiting for us.

It Is My Intention to Make
My Entire Life a Rejection of War

———————

Merton's life of prayer, and the disciplined practice of writing that accompanied it, led him to become a prophet of peace to the world of war. If he didn't enter the monastery with the intention of becoming a best-selling author, he certainly did not set out to be a prophet either. His daily meditation and liturgical prayer, his ongoing scripture reading, his silent opening to the void before God, combined with his spectacular gifts as a writer and intellectual, made him a fluid receptacle for God's wisdom. He came along just at the right moment after World War II, as millions of people faced the failures of the world and the despair for any real nonviolent global change. Just at that moment, Merton appeared on the scene with his unusual story of spiritual conversion and spiritual invitation. He spoke an authentic word about the spiritual life and found a receptive national and international audience.

For twenty-seven years, Merton listened attentively in contemplative silence for the God of peace and he diligently shared with the world what he heard and learned. That's the definition of a prophet. A prophet is one who takes quality time to be present to God and to listen to whatever God has to say, and then shares what God has to say with the world, whether the world wants to hear it or not, and even whether the prophet wants to share it or not. God is a God of peace, Merton discovered, and this God of peace wants us to live in peace, truth, love, compassion, and wisdom. That was a message Merton had to share with the entire world.

In a world of total violence, systemic injustice, and permanent war, such news is never well received. The world wants a god of war who blesses our wars, a god of money who helps us to win the lottery, a god of winners who makes sure we get ahead of others. We prefer to keep the real God under control, locked up in church, so that we can go along with our wars, corporate greed, and imperial ambitions.

Merton sought the true living God. He let the consequences of that spiritual commitment unfold as they would, including rejection by many of his fellow monks and other Catholics. It was inevitable that this great soul would eventually address the idolatries and blasphemies of war and nuclear weapons.

Merton announced that the spiritual life requires creative nonviolence, that we cannot authentically claim to worship the God of peace and still support the false gods of war. This political word from a spiritual master was a great gift, but came at great cost to Merton in ways we may never know or understand. For me, that's the sign of an authentic Christian in our midst. It's the path before any authentic seeker. All those who study and emulate Merton will eventually speak out against war, nuclear weapons, and global violence, and will suffer real consequences for their truth-telling. As more and more of us listen in prayerful contemplation to the word of the God of peace, more and more of us will be compelled to stand up and speak out in prophetic witness as Merton did.

In the mid-1960s, Merton wrote a dramatic statement explaining how he hoped his entire life would stand in sharp contrast to the culture of war and violence. It not only reveals the depth of his spiritual and political beliefs, it challenges us to reflect on our own lives and our relationship to the culture of war and violence.

> To adopt a life that is essentially non-assertive, a nonviolent life of humility and peace, is in itself a statement of one's position. But each one in such a life can, by the personal modality of his decision, give his whole life a special orientation.

ॐ

It is my intention to make my entire life a rejection of, a protest against the crimes and injustices of war and political tyranny which threaten to destroy the whole human race and the world.

ॐ

By my monastic life and vows, I am saying no to all the concentration camps, the aerial bombardments, the staged political trials, the judicial murders, the racial injustices, the economic tyrannies, and the whole socio-economic apparatus which seems geared for nothing but global destruction in spite of all its fair words in favor of peace. I make my monastic silence a protest against the lies of politicians, propagandists and agitators, and when I speak it is to deny that my faith and my Church can ever seriously be aligned with these forces of injustice and destruction.

ॐ

My life, then, must be a protest against [those who invoke their faith in support of war, racial injustice, and tyranny] also, and perhaps against these most of all. . . . The time has come for judgment to be passed on this history. I can rejoice in this fact, believing that the judgment will be a liberation of Christian faith from servitude to and involvement in the structures of the secular world.

ॐ

If I say no to all these secular forces, I also say yes to all that is good in the world and in humanity. I say yes to all that is beautiful in nature. . . . I say yes to all the men and women who are my brothers and sisters in the world.[1]

ॐ

Merton's stand against the culture of war is a great gift and a great challenge. He inspires me to make my life "a rejection of and a protest against the crimes and injustices of war and political tyranny which continue to threaten the whole human race and the earth itself." With Merton, I want to say No to every form of violence—nuclear weapons, executions, handguns, Trident submarines, torture, imprisonment, corporate greed, poverty, hunger, occupation, imperialism, and environmental destruction. With Merton, I want to say Yes to everything that is peaceful, holy, loving, and of God—nature, creation, all creatures, all human beings, all that is good. I think he invites all those of goodwill to take such a prophetic stand.

Merton shows us that no matter what our state in life we can take a public stand against war and violence, and for peace and nonviolence. He urges us through his humble circumstances to take our own prophetic stand. I hear him whisper quietly, "Walk away from the culture of war, turn back to the God of peace, embrace everyone as sister and brother, live at one with creation, enter the communion of peace, enjoy the fullness of life in nonviolence, let love and compassion reign."

This consistent prophetic stand should exemplify the ordinary, public stand of the Christian in today's world of permanent war. "If one reads the prophets with ears and eyes open," Merton wrote to Daniel Berrigan in 1962, "then you cannot help recognizing our obligation to shout very loud about God's will, God's truth, and God's justice."[2] "I am against war, against violence, against violent revolution, for peaceful settlement of differences, for nonviolent but nevertheless radical change," Merton wrote to a friend shortly before his death.

"I am on the side of the people who are being burned, bombed, cut to pieces, tortured, held as hostages, gassed, ruined and destroyed," Merton wrote in the 1960s. "They are the victims of both sides. To take sides with massive power is to take sides against the innocent. The side I take is the side of the people who are sick of war and who want peace, who want to rebuild their lives and their countries and the world."[3] Merton challenges us to take sides—to side with the poor and the children; with the innocent; with our enemies; to side with peace, justice, and nonviolence; to side with the God of peace and justice.

Just as Merton learned to make his life a rejection of war and a public cry for peace, we, too, can make our lives a rejection and protest against war, injustice, and nuclear weapons and become prophets of nonviolence to the culture of violence, or at least, a prophetic community of peace.

How can we carry on Merton's prophetic work? What would it mean for us to speak that prophetic message today? I think it means saying as clearly, lovingly, and publicly as we can, something like this: "In the name of the God of peace, the time of war is over. God's reign of peace is at hand. Start practicing and teaching nonviolence." This message will not be well received, as Merton's peace message was by and large rejected. But we must say it, and we must be specific. Here are other ways to say our message:

> In the name of the God of peace, we need to close all U.S. military bases at home and abroad. We need to close the Los Alamos Nuclear Weapons Labs, Livermore Labs, the SAC base, Vandenberg Air Force Base, the Oak Ridge Nuclear Weapons Center, West Point, the CIA, the NSA, and the Pentagon. We need to undertake treaties for total nuclear disarmament, join the World Court, obey international law, sign the Kyoto accord, find alternatives to fossil fuels, stop global warming, end the Star Wars program, cut the military budget, and abolish every nuclear weapon, Trident sub, and weapon of mass destruction. Then, with the trillions of dollars left over, feed every starving child and refugee on the planet immediately. Work to end extreme poverty. Give food, housing, health care, education, employment, and dignity to every human being, and educate every child on the planet in the methodology of nonviolent conflict resolution. Clean up the earth, end environmental destruction, protect all creatures and all creation, and institutionalize nonviolent conflict resolution programs everywhere so that war becomes obsolete and peace can begin to reign at home and abroad.

This is what Merton would say today. Like Merton, we too can listen to the God of peace and go forth into the culture of war to announce God's word of peace and nonviolence, come what may. This may be the highest calling of all, and it's certainly the most needed. If we get rejected, that just gives us another opportunity to practice gospel nonviolence. If the message gets accepted, then we can rejoice in the blessing of God. Either way, God's will and word will be served. In the end, with Merton, that's what's first and foremost.

If Only They Could All See Themselves as They Really Are

———————

Merton was constantly working on himself. He wanted the world to change, so he tried to change himself, to grow spiritually, to open his heart wider before God. The difference with Merton is that he kept trying to change. He never gave up changing himself. He went to Asia in pursuit of conversion and transformation. This is a rare trait, requiring painful, strenuous effort.

Merton was willing to be converted, not just once but many times over. We miss the point of Merton's life if we stop at his famous conversion to Catholicism and entrance into the monastery. Merton's life was a series of ongoing conversions, large and small. He demonstrates that a true spiritual seeker, a real peacemaker, is a person who undergoes many conversions, many changes, many transformations throughout one's life. Indeed, for Merton, life is a series of conversions and transformations that prepare us for the ultimate transformation of death and resurrection.

The 1958 revelation on the street corner in downtown Louisville, Kentucky, is certainly one of his most well-known turning points. While standing at a busy intersection, he suddenly saw everyone through the loving eyes of God and realized that he loved all these people. As simple as this sounds, it was a huge breakthrough for him. Like most monks, priests, and religious, Merton had internalized the myth that he was different from other people. He was "subtly" superior to them because he had withdrawn from the world and its sins and chosen the higher ground of prayer, solitude, and monasticism. But standing on that Louisville street corner, Merton let this simple, sudden, stunning realization change him. Unlike others, he welcomed transformation. He wanted to improve, to become more loving, more compassionate, more nonviolent, more Godly. Scholars say that afterward, he began to reach out to more and more people through his correspondence and got actively involved in the pressing issues of the day. The experience is told in *Conjectures of a Guilty Bystander*:

> In Louisville, at the corner of Fourth and Walnut, in the center of the shopping district, I was suddenly overwhelmed with the realization that I loved all these people, that they were mine and I theirs, that we could not be alien to one another even though we were total strangers. It was like waking from a dream of separateness, of spurious self-isolation in a special world, the world of renunciation and supposed holiness. The whole illusion of a separate holy existence is a dream.

> This sense of liberation from an illusory difference was such a relief and such a joy to me that I almost laughed out loud. And I suppose my happiness could have taken form in these words: "Thank God, thank God, that I am like others, that I am only a man among others. . . ." It is a glorious destiny to be a member of the human race, though it is a race dedicated to many absurdities and one which makes many terrible mistakes: yet, with all that, God Himself gloried in becoming a member of the human race. A member of the human race! To think that such a commonplace realization should suddenly seem like news that one holds the winning ticket in a cosmic sweepstake.

> I have the immense joy of being human, a member of the human race in which God Himself became incarnate. As if

the sorrows and stupidities of the human condition could overwhelm me, now I realize what we all are. And if only everybody could realize this! But it cannot be explained. There is no way of telling people that they are all walking around shining like the sun. . . . There are no strangers!

❧

Then it was as if I suddenly saw the secret beauty of their heart, the depths of their hearts where neither sin nor desire nor self-knowledge can reach, the core of their reality, the person that each one is in God's eyes. If only they could all see themselves as they really are. If only we could see each other that way all the time. There would be no more war, no more hatred, no more cruelty, no more greed. . . . I suppose the big problem would be that we would fall down and worship each other. . . . The gate of heaven is everywhere.[1]

❧

Merton's awakening to universal, compassionate love for every human being is at the heart of peacemaking and the spiritual life. Sooner or later, all spiritual seekers, all peacemakers, recognize that we are all one, that we are already united, that we are all children of the God of peace, that we are all therefore sisters and brothers of one another. This is the core truth of reality, that we are all one. It takes a long spiritual practice and the grace of God to open our eyes to this truth of our common unity, but once it is realized and accepted with all one's heart and being, there is no turning back. One reaches out in love toward every human being, and does whatever one can to stop the killing, suffering, injustice, and wars that tear apart our sisters and brothers. Indeed, the real problem involves fighting the temptation to fall down in worship before others because we recognize the presence of God in every human being and see everyone now as our beloved sister and brother.

Of course, every monk, priest, Christian, and religious person should see life through the eyes of universal love, compassion, and peace. Alas, this insight is slow in coming for us all. While Merton knew this, glimpsed it, and wrote about it, he fully realized and embraced it here, not in the safe confines of the monastery, but on a busy street intersection in downtown Louisville.

Merton's awakening and his moving account of it invite each one of us to ponder our own attitude toward the human race. When did we wake up and realize that every human being is our sister and brother? How do we rejoice in being a member of the human race? How do we live out the truth that we are one with every human being, that we are all children of the God of peace? How does this spiritual truth push us to reach out in love toward everyone and work for a world where there is "no more war, no more hatred, no more cruelty, and no more greed"?

Thomas Merton invites us to pursue conversion and transformation with the same vigor that he did. His story confirms for us the wisdom that it is better to open ourselves to conversion and transformation, and not to run from them. We need not live in fear of change; we should embrace it as the Spirit of God moving through us. Conversion and transformation, especially when it widens our hearts to embrace every human being in universal, compassionate, nonviolent love, is a great blessing, the blessing of all blessings to be prayed for and sought.

Note also Merton's humility in sharing this spiritual experience. He could have kept it to himself. He did not have to write about it. By doing so, he not only shows us his limitation—his secret belief that he was above everyone else—he shows how wrong he was, and how happy he was to realize his grievous spiritual error. This humility and the sharing of his experience are both part of the conversion and transformation. By telling his story and confessing his Phariseeism, he inspires us to break through our own narrow sense of superiority, entitlement, and privilege, into the realization that we are one with all people, that we are called to love all people, and that God is the loving Creator of all people, including ordinary us.

9

Blessed Are the Nonviolent

On August 21, 1962, Thomas Merton decided to get serious about nonviolence. "Today I realize with urgency the absolute seriousness of my need to study and practice nonviolence," he wrote in his journal on August 21, 1962. He continued,

Hitherto, I have "liked" nonviolence as an idea. I have "approved" it, looked with benignity on it, have praised it, even earnestly. But I have not practiced it fully. My thoughts and words retaliate. I condemn and resist adversaries when I think I am unjustly treated. I revile them, even treat them with open (but polite) contempt to their face. This restricting non-retaliation merely to physical non-retaliation is not enough—on the contrary, it is in some sense a greater evil. At the same time, the energy wasted in contempt, criticism and resentment is thus diverted from its true function—insistence on truth. Hence loss of clarity, loss of focus, confusion, and finally frustration. I need to set myself to the study of nonviolence, with thoroughness. The completely, integral practice of it in community. Eventually teaching it to others by word and example.[1]

Merton did take up the study of nonviolence. He published many articles and some significant books, such as *Gandhi on Nonviolence*, but only after very serious study and note taking. He also began to work on his inner violence, particularly his resentment and hostility toward members of his community.

Further, he began meeting frequently with peace movement organizers and joining various peace and justice organizations.

By 1966 he was ready to teach nonviolence with greater wisdom and authority. He accepted an invitation from the Fellowship of Reconciliation to publish an extended essay on Christian nonviolence. His essay "Blessed Are the Meek: The Christian Roots of Nonviolence" was first published as a pamphlet and dedicated to Joan Baez, before eventually appearing in various books.

"Christian nonviolence is not built on a presupposed division, but on the basic unity of humanity." That's the first insight Merton announces in his visionary essay. We are all one, and because we are all one, because we are all sisters and brothers of one another, we would never hurt or kill anyone, much less sit still while billions suffer war, poverty, injustice, and catastrophic climate change. Because we are all one, because we recognize every human being as our very sister or brother, we reach out with active love toward everyone, reconcile with everyone, disarm everyone, make peace with everyone, and do our best to end the suffering and violence and to welcome God's reign of peace and nonviolence. That's the foundation of Jesus's sermon, Merton's life, and all we do for peace.

"Blessed Are the Meek" is a profound meditation on Christian nonviolence. It takes a lifetime to understand the depth of Merton's wisdom. He roots all Christian nonviolence, first of all, in Christ and Christ's reign of peace. Though he never says it explicitly, he knows Christ is the epitome of nonviolence, and Christ's realm is a reign of nonviolence that welcomes all human beings—and that as servants and disciples of the nonviolent Christ, we, too, therefore, practice nonviolence, serve his reign of nonviolence, and give our lives for the disarmament of the world. He explains,

> Nonviolence is not simply a way of proving one's point and getting what one wants without being involved in behavior that one considers ugly and evil. Nor is it, for that matter, a means which anyone legitimately can make use of according to his fancy for any purpose whatever. To practice

nonviolence for a purely selfish or arbitrary end would in fact discredit and distort the truth of nonviolent resistance.

&

Nonviolence is perhaps the most exacting of all forms of struggle, not only because it demands first of all that one be ready to suffer evil and even face the threat of death without violent retaliation, but because it excludes mere transient self-interest from its considerations. In a very real sense, the one who practices nonviolent resistance must commit himself not to the defense of his own interests or even those of a particular group: he must commit himself to the defense of objective truth and right and above all, of humanity.[2]

Merton's nonviolence demands complete selflessness. Nonviolent resisters place humanity first and foremost, and by that he means the truth of our common unity in God. Because we serve humanity with unconditional, active love, we give our lives for humanity, even to the point of accepting suffering without retaliating, even unto imprisonment and death, all for the disarmament, healing, and reconciliation of the human race and creation.

For the Christian, this way of selfless nonviolent action on behalf of suffering humanity is modeled by Christ. He continues,

For the Christian, the basis of nonviolence is the Gospel message of salvation for all men and women and of the Kingdom of God to which all are summoned. The disciple of Christ, the one who has heard the good news, the announcement of the Lord's coming and of His victory, and is aware of the definitive establishment of the Kingdom, proves his faith by the gift of his whole self to the Lord in order that all may enter the Kingdom. This Christian discipleship entails a certain way of acting which is proper to the Kingdom.

∾

The religious basis for Christian nonviolence is faith in Christ the Redeemer and obedience to his demand to love and manifest himself in us by a certain manner of acting in the world and in relation to other men and women. This obedience enables us to live as true citizens of the Kingdom, in which the divine mercy, the grace, favor and redeeming love of God are active in our lives. Then the Holy Spirit will indeed "rest upon us" and act in us, not for our own good alone but for God and God's Kingdom. And if the Spirit dwells in us and works in us, our lives will be a continuous and progressive conversion and transformation in which we also, in some measure, help to transform others and allow ourselves to be transformed by and with others—in Christ.[3]

Christian nonviolence flows naturally from discipleship and obedience to the nonviolent Christ, to allegiance to his reign of nonviolence to becoming instruments of God's spirit disarming the world, Merton explains. For the Christian there is no other choice or option: Christians are nonviolent because Christ is nonviolent. That means, therefore, that no Christian who claims to follow the nonviolent Christ can support war, handguns, nuclear weapons, or violence of any kind. Further, Christians renounce any allegiance to the world of violence because their focus remains on God's reign of nonviolence. This obedience and allegiance open us completely so that the Holy Spirit can use us for its healing work.

Christian nonviolence, for Merton, was eschatological. This theological understanding of our work for peace is new, and all Christian peacemakers need to ponder it. "Eschatology" means literally "the study of the last things." From a Christian perspective, it means the study of the end-times, the judgment, and the coming of God. When seen through the lens of gospel nonviolence, it takes on great hope but also great urgency. For

Merton, then, eschatological nonviolence becomes the way to understand our problems and our way out:

> Christian meekness, which is essential to true nonviolence, has [an] eschatological quality about it. It refrains from self-assertion and from violent aggression because it sees all things in the light of the great judgment. Hence it does not struggle and fight merely for this or that ephemeral gain. It struggles for the truth and the right which alone will stand in that day when all is to be tried by fire.
>
> Christian nonviolence and meekness imply a particular understanding of the power of human poverty and powerlessness when they are united with the invisible strength of Christ. The Beatitudes indeed convey a profound existential understanding of the dynamic of the Kingdom of God.... This is a dynamism of patient and secret growth, in belief that out of the smallest, weakest, and most insignificant seed the greatest tree will come.... Christian nonviolence is rooted in this consciousness and this faith.
>
> This aspect of Christian nonviolence is extremely important and it gives us the key to a proper understanding of the meekness which accepts being "without strength" not out of masochism, quietism, defeatism or false passivity, but trusting in the strength of the Lord of truth. Indeed, we repeat, Christian nonviolence is nothing if not first of all a formal profession of faith in the Gospel message that the Kingdom has been established and that the Lord of truth is indeed risen and reigning over his Kingdom.[4]

Merton insists that Christian nonviolence rests solely on Christ, on his reign, on his resurrection, and therefore on the truth of his reign coming to earth in its present fullness of loving nonviolence. This insight means that Christians focus on the nonviolent Christ, his reign and resurrection, and give themselves to welcoming that reign of peace on earth and witnessing to his resurrection over death, however small, helpless, and powerless we may seem. This is precisely the methodology of God to manifest God's reign. As disciples of the nonviolent Christ, we serve his reign, resurrection, and nonviolence, pure and simple, even if it seems we are unsuccessful, ineffective, or irrelevant, which is probably what will happen.

Christians have failed to do this because of bad theology. Their "eschatology" leaves them living for the afterlife. The difference for Merton is that Christian peacemakers have what he called a "realized eschatology," which focuses on the here and now. In his journal at the time, he wrote that peacemakers need to develop this understanding of "realized eschatology" to help them through the urgent imperative of nonviolent living in the here and now, no matter how small their numbers might be. He wrote,

> The concept of realized eschatology is very important. It means the transformation of life and of human relations by Christ *now* (rather than an eschatology focused on future cosmic and religious events). Realized eschatology is at the heart of a genuine Christian (incarnational) humanism. Hence, its tremendous importance for the Christian peace effort, for example. The presence of the Holy Spirit, the call to repentance, the call to see Christ in humanity, the presence of the redeeming power of the cross in the sacraments. These belong to the "last age," in which we now are. But all these do not reveal their significance without a Christian peacemaking mission, without the preaching of the gospel of unity, nonviolence and mercy: the reconciliation of people with people and therefore with God. This duty does not mean, however, that there will not at the same time be great revolutionary upheaval. The preaching of peace by a tiny remnant in an age of war and violence is one of the eschatological signs of the true life of the church. By the activity of the church as peacemaker, the work of God will be mysteriously accomplished in the world.[5]

In *Seeds of Destruction*, Merton extrapolated on the eschatological implications of Christian nonviolence and peacemaking:

> The Christian is and must be by his or her very adoption as a son or daughter of God, in Christ, a peacemaker. He or

she is bound to imitate the Savior, who, instead of defending himself with twelve legions of angels (Mt. 26:55), allowed himself to be nailed to the cross and died praying for his executioners. The Christian is one whose life has sprung from a particular spiritual seed: the blood of the martyrs who, without offering forcible resistance, laid down their lives rather than submit to the unjust laws that demanded an official religious cult of the emperor as God.

One verse in St. John's account of the Passion of Christ makes clear the underlying principles of war and peace in the Gospel (John 18:36). Questioned by Pilate as to whether he is a king, Jesus replies, "My kingdom is not of this world," and explains that if he were a worldly king his followers would be fighting for him. In other words, the Christian attitude to war and peace is fundamentally eschatological. The Christian does not need to fight and indeed it is better that he should not fight, for in so far as he imitates his lord and master, he proclaims that the Messianic kingdom has come and bears witness to the presence of the *Kyrios Pantocrator* in mystery, even in the midst of the conflicts and turmoil of the world.

The book of the New Testament that definitely canonizes this eschatological view of peace in the midst of spiritual combat is Revelation (the Apocalypse), which sets forth in mysterious and symbolic language the critical struggle of the nascent church with the powers of the world, as typified by the Roman Empire. This struggle, which is definitive and marks the last age of the world, is the final preparation for the manifestation of Christ as Lord of the Universe.

The kingdom is already present in the world, since Christ has overcome the world and risen from the dead. But the kingdom is still not fully manifested and remains outwardly powerless. It is a kingdom of saints and martyrs, priests and witnesses, whose main function is to bide their time in faith, loving one another and the truth, suffering persecution in the furious cataclysm which marks the final testing of earthly society. They will take no direct part in the struggles of earthly kingdoms. Their life is one of faith, gentleness, meekness, patience, purity. They depend on no power other than the power of God, and it is God they obey rather than the state, which tends to usurp the powers of God and to blaspheme him.[6]

With these biblical insights into an eschatological understanding of the times we live in, Merton helps us to carry on the work of peace and the way of nonviolence, knowing that we are fulfilling God's work in the world, in salvation history. This is at once intensely demanding but also liberating. All we have to do is our part as peacemakers following the peacemaking Christ. We rely solely on the God of peace and live fully in the Kingdom of God right now.

In the main section of "Blessed Are the Meek," Merton offers several key "conditions for relative honesty in the practice of Christian nonviolence":

- Nonviolence must be aimed above all at the transformation of the present state of the world.
- The nonviolent resistance of the Christian who belongs to one of the powerful nations and who is himself in some sense a privileged member of world society will have to be clearly not *for himself* but *for others*—that is, for the poor and underprivileged.
- In the case of the nonviolent struggle for peace, the threat of nuclear war abolishes all privileges. Nonviolence must avoid self-righteousness.
- Nonviolence must avoid the fetishism of immediate visible results. The realism of nonviolence must be made evident by humility and self-restraint that clearly show frankness and open-mindedness and invite the adversary to serious and reasonable discussion. The nonviolent resister is persuaded of the superior efficacy of love, openness, peaceful negotiation, and above all, truth.
- Christian nonviolence is convinced that the manner in which the conflict for truth is waged will itself manifest or obscure the truth. The absolute refusal of evil or suspect means is a necessary element in the witness of nonviolence.

- Nonviolence requires a willingness to learn something from the adversary. Our readiness to see some good in him and to agree with some of his ideas actually gives us power—the power of sincerity and truth. This mission of Christian humility in social life is not merely to edify but to keep minds open to many alternatives. The rigidity of a certain type of Christian thought has seriously impaired this capacity, which nonviolence must recover.

- The quality of nonviolence is decided largely by the purity of the Christian hope behind it. If the Christian hopes that God will grant peace to the world, it is because he also trusts that humanity, God's creature, is not basically evil: that there is in humanity a potentiality for peace and order that can be realized, given the right conditions. Despair is not permitted to the meek, the humble, the afflicted, the ones famished for justice, the merciful, the clean of heart and the peacemakers. The meekness and humility that Christ extolled in the Sermon on the Mount and that are the basis of true Christian nonviolence are inseparable from an eschatological Christian hope that is completely open to the presence of God in the world and therefore to the presence of our brother or sister who is always seen, no matter who he or she may be, in the perspectives of the Kingdom. The hope of the Christian must be like the hope of a child, pure and full of trust. The humility of Christian nonviolence is at once patient and uncalculating.[7]

In these sublime teachings, Merton reminds us that the focus of our active nonviolence is the disarmament of the world itself. That means, we side with the poor and underprivileged, renouncing any self-righteousness because we are, by definition, overprivileged. We let go of the rush for tangible results, remaining steady and faithful to the work and witness of nonviolence, remembering that the ends lie within the means, that the means are already the ends. Our nonviolence therefore requires an openness and humility before our adversary, and steadfast hope in Christ, God the Creator, and humanity. We never give in to despair, because our eyes are fixed on the nonviolent reign of

God, which is real, and at the same time, coming to earth. So we go forward in hope, practicing active nonviolence; doing what we can with others for the abolition of war, poverty, nuclear weapons, and all violence; and trusting that God is using us to achieve God's goals.

"The key to nonviolence," Merton concludes, "is the willingness of the nonviolent resister to suffer a certain amount of accidental evil in order to bring about a change of mind in the oppressor and awaken him to personal openness and to dialogue."[8] [QY] Merton's nonviolence is active, open, humble, steadfast, truthful, hopeful, eschatological, and redemptive. In the end, we willingly accept suffering without any desire for retaliation in our pursuit of justice and disarmament, as the nonviolent Jesus teaches us, knowing that nonviolent suffering love is always redemptive and transformative. Merton invites every Christian to reclaim the nonviolence of Christ and our own nonviolence, which lies hidden, innate within each one of us. If we lived out these guidelines, not only would there be fewer wars and less violence, we would be closer in our discipleship to Christ. We might actually become authentic Christians.

Merton summed up his vision of nonviolence in his essay "Peace and Revolution":

> Nonviolence is not for power but for truth. It is not pragmatic but prophetic. It is not aimed at immediate political results, but at the manifestation of fundamental and crucially important truth. Nonviolence is not primarily the language of efficacy, but the language of Kairos. It does not say, "We shall overcome," so much as, "This is the day of the Lord, and whatever may happen to us, He shall overcome."[9]

Nonviolence for Merton is always focused on the nonviolent Jesus and his reign of nonviolence. No matter how far along we get in the struggle for disarmament and justice, we keep our focus on the nonviolent Jesus and remember that this is his work. We follow the nonviolent Jesus and serve his reign of nonviolence, trusting in faith, hope, and love that "he shall overcome," that a new world of nonviolence is at hand.

10

The Silence and Solitude of Peace

Merton spent his monastic life in contemplative silence and daily solitude like a Gandhian *satyagrahi* (a nonviolent soldier of truth force) and Zen master set on God, determined to dwell in the presence of God, even if that presence took the form of absence. I think that this life of silence and solitude, which he sought so diligently and wrote about so well, led his searching spirit to unpack the social, economic, and political implications of God's peace. It helped me make the connections, see more clearly, and speak out fearlessly about the violence of our time.

Merton could outline the vision of nonviolence with such power and authority because he first went deep into the contemplative life of prayerful nonviolence. He insisted that silence and solitude were necessary prerequisites that could lead us deeper into peace and the God of peace, that we might be healed of violence, learn how to love everyone, reclaim our common unity with one another and creation, and encounter the living God of peace.

"It is in deep solitude that I find the gentleness with which I can truly love my brothers and sisters," Merton wrote in his journal on January 12, 1950. "The more solitary I am, the more affection I have for them. It is pure affection, and filled with reverence for the solitude of others. Solitude and silence teach me to love my brothers and sisters for what they are, not for what they say. . . . Solitude is not merely a negative relationship. It is not merely the absence of people or of presence with people. True solitude is a participation in the solitariness of God Who is in all things."[1]

Silence and solitude open a way to gentleness, love, and God, Merton teaches. Through his daily silence and solitude, Merton showed us how to renounce our inner violence and the world's violence, let go of our resentments and hatred, make peace with ourselves, enter the nonviolence of God, and open our hearts with love and compassion toward all beings and all creation. The faithful practice of silence and solitude can take us deeper into the silence and solitude of God, he testified. From there, we can reach out with greater loving nonviolence toward all humanity and all creation.

Shortly after moving into his hermitage, Merton wrote, "What more do I seek than this silence, this simplicity, this 'living together with wisdom'? For me there is nothing else. Last night, before going to bed, I realized momentarily what solitude really means: when the ropes are cast off and the skiff is no longer tied to the land, but heads out to sea without ties, without restraints! Not the sea of passion; on the contrary, the sea of purity and love that is without care, that loves God alone, immediately and directly in Himself as the All (and the seeming Nothing that is all)."[2] That same week he summed up the goal of his life: "to be one of those who entirely practices contemplation simply in order to follow Christ."[3]

"The great joy of the solitary life is not found simply in quiet, in the beauty and peace of nature, the song of birds, etc., nor in the peace of one's own heart," Merton wrote.

[It's] in the awakening and attuning of the heart to the voice of God—to the inexplicable, quite definite inner certitude of one's call to obey God, to hear God, to worship God here, now, today, in silence and alone, and that this is the whole reason for one's existence, this makes one's existence fruitful and gives fruitfulness to all one's other good acts, and is the ransom and purification of one's heart, which has been dead in sin. It is not simply a question of "existing" alone, but of doing, with joy and understanding, "the work of the cell," which is done in silence and not according to one's own choice or the pressure of necessity, but in obedience to God. But the voice of God is not "heard" at every moment, and part of the "work of the cell" is attention so that one may not miss any sound of that Voice.[4]

We need not become monks or hermits to seek God, but Merton's strenuous silence and solitude remind us that silence and solitude are necessary ingredients for the journey to peace and the God of peace. He reminds us to take quiet time in solitude every day to open ourselves up to God and God's gift of peace. If we take quality time every day to retreat from our busy lives, enter into silence and solitude, acknowledge the presence of God, and recenter ourselves in God's peace, we will discover new strength to go forth in a gentle, nonviolent, loving spirit to face our day and the world of violence. More, we will discover new wisdom and grace to follow the nonviolent Jesus and witness to God's reign of peace.

The peace of silence and solitude opens up space for us to befriend ourselves, love ourselves, and accept ourselves. As we make peace with ourselves, get to know ourselves, and understand our restless minds, we breathe easier and receive new gifts of peace. As we encounter ourselves in peaceful solitude, practice mindfulness, and treat ourselves nonviolently, we begin to love ourselves, which allows us to move forward with love toward others and God. Dwelling in peace helps us to live in peace and prepares us to dwell in the peace of God and to make peace with everyone.

In the solitude of peace, we notice the depths of the violence within us, but also the depths of peace. We can sit in quiet peace and reflect upon the violence we suffered as children from our families, school classmates, and the world at large. In this safe place of peace, we realize the many ways we have not been loved by family or friends or the world. We see anew how we have been victimized by violence, how we have been hurt and wounded, how this violence has led to deep-seated resentment and anger, and how we have made peace with violence. We can recognize the ways we have responded to violence with violence, and reject those ways. There, in the solitude of peace, the God of peace can come to us privately, touch us, love us, heal us, and disarm us. In the solitude of peace, we can dwell in peace, cultivate interior peace, and return to the sanity of peace and nonviolence.

When we sit in contemplative prayer, we enter the presence of the God of peace, and allow God to dig out the roots of violence within us and give us the gift of peace, that we might become God's peacemakers. We cultivate an interior nonviolence. We welcome Christ's resurrection gift of peace. And we find ourselves sent fearlessly, lovingly, hopefully into the world of war with the good news of God's peace.

Solitude helps us grow in awareness of the present moment, and trains us to live more consciously in the present moment. Through this mindful awareness of the present moment, which we relearn every day in our solitude, we come alive and live in the fullness of life. Interestingly, it can also help us get ready to accept our deaths with peace. "Solitude is life," Merton writes. "It aims not at a living death but at a certain fullness of life. But a fullness that comes from honestly and authentically facing death and accepting it without care, with faith and trust in God."[5]

Solitude can help us become gentler, Merton discovered. Here in a 1953 journal entry he describes the fruits of solitude. "A gentleness, a silence, a humility that I have never had before, which seems impossible in the community where even my compassion is tinged with force and strain. If I am called to solitude, it is, I think, to unlearn all tension, and get rid of the strain that has always falsified me in the presence of others and put harshness into the words of my mind."[6]

Thomas Merton invites us into the solitude of peace as a safe place to open our hearts to the God of peace and let God give us God's gift of peace. I recommend twenty, thirty, or sixty minutes a day in silent meditation with the God of peace every morning for every Christian peacemaker. In this quiet, ordinary, daily experience, we sit with the God of peace, with the nonviolent Jesus, in our ordinary world, with our ordinary brokenness and confusion. It's simply a matter of showing up, being there, opening ourselves, and attending regularly to the presence of God. If we dare show up regularly, God can't resist. The God of peace who wants to give us peace will make peace with us and transform us into God's peacemakers. If we remain faithful to silence and solitude, and the prayer of contemplative peace and nonviolence, we will receive new strength and grace to make peace in the world of war.

11

Hermit for Peace

In search of greater solitude, Merton moved into the woods and became one of the first official hermits in the modern history of the Cistercian Order. In one stroke, he reclaimed an ancient spiritual tradition, discovered a new opening for personal growth, and took a radical stand against the culture of consumerism, materialism, and violence. Like Thoreau, he chose to "live deliberately," to go deeper into silence, prayer, nature, and peace. From day one, he was not disappointed.

The monastery began building Merton's little cinderblock house in 1959 a mile from the church. Initially, it was intended as a conference center, but Merton soon named it a hermitage. He received permission to spend several hours a day up there alone. Then in August 1965 he said good-bye to the community, taught his last theology class for the scholastics, and moved in permanently. His intention was to sever ties with the world and to open himself as radically as possible to God. At first he went up to the monastery once a day for Mass and a meal. After a while, he seems to have gone up to the monastery just once a week for Mass or to give a talk, which was open to any community member.

Merton's hermitage is not at all remarkable. A plain cinderblock house with a large open porch made of a concrete floor, it looks out over a beautiful green lawn that slopes down into a gentle valley. Surrounded by trees, birds, rabbits, and deer, its location is hidden away and peaceful. Upon entering there's a large room with a gray stone fireplace, a wooden rocking chair, bookshelves, and a large wooden desk, where Merton wrote and looked out over the valley. In the back, there's a little kitchen, bathroom, bedroom, and a small chapel.

For someone who never owned his own home, much less a car, TV, or much money before he entered, this little house in the woods was nothing less than a gift from God. For the first time, Merton tasted the freedom of having his own home. He was free of the monastery, free to make his own schedule, free to sit in peace. For the first time in ages, he felt happy.

During those first days, he was filled with consolation, with a sense of peace and joy he had not known since entering the monastery in 1941. His initial journal entries confess his peace and joy.

> Everything about this hermitage fills me with gladness. There are lots of things that could have been far more perfect one way or the other, ascetically or domestically, but it is the place God has given me after so much prayer and longing and without my deserving it, and it is a delight. I can imagine no other joy on earth than to have such a place to be at peace in. To live in silence, to think and write, to listen to the wind and to all the voices of the wood, to struggle with a new anguish, which is nevertheless, blessed and secure, to live in the shadow of a big cedar cross, to prepare for my death and my exodus to the heavenly country, to love my brothers and all people, to pray for the whole world and offer peace and good sense among people. So it is my place in the scheme of things and that is sufficient. Amen.[1]

> The five days I have had in real solitude have been a revelation, and whatever questions I may have had about it before are now answered. Over and over again, I see that this life is what I have always hoped it would be and always sought. It is a life of peace, silence, purpose and meaning. Certainly it is not easy. It always calls for a blessed and salutary effort, but a little of this goes a long way. Everything about this life is rewarding.[2]

᷃

No question whatever that this is the kind of schedule to live by. I went down to say Mass and will go down again for dinner. The rest of the time here does not begin to be enough. How full the days are. Full and slow and quiet. Ordered, occupied (sawing wood, sweeping, reading, taking notes, meditating, praying, tending the fire or just looking at the valley). Only here do I feel that my life is fully human. And only what is authentically human is fit to be offered to God.[3]

᷃

There is no question for me that my one job as a monk is to live this hermit life in simple direct contact with nature, primitively, quietly, doing some writing, maintaining such contacts as are willed by God and bearing witness to the value and goodness of simple things and ways, loving God in all of it. I am more convinced of this than of anything else in my life and I am sure it is what God asks of me.[4]

᷃

What more do I seek than this silence, this simplicity, this "living together with wisdom"? For me, there is nothing else, and to think that I had the grace to taste a little of what all men and women really seek without realizing it! All the more obligation to have compassion and love, and to pray for them.[5]

Today, everyone is caught up in the rat race of competition, consumerism, and noise. The violence around us seeps into us, eats away at us, and destroys us even without our knowing it. We grow ever more unconscious. Few people seem hopeful, happy, peaceful, or joyful.

Alone in the woods with his prayer books, Merton shows us that we need not give in to violence, that we can create a life of nonviolence for ourselves, that we can reclaim our humanity, that we can be at peace with ourselves through daily prayer, quiet meditation, scripture study, and solitude. We can live at peace, he insists. We can make peace with the God of peace, with creation, with humanity. What's more, we need to do this. This is our best hope.

Merton's solitary life as a poor hermit on the grounds of the monastery stands in contrast to the world of Twitter, Facebook, and iPhones—not to mention gun shootings, widespread hunger, drone bombings, nuclear weapons, corporate greed, and catastrophic climate change. While the rest of the world was charged with racism, war, consumerism, nuclear weapons, and the war on communism, Merton stood like a nonviolent desert father in northern Egypt, in total opposition to the empire. He refused to give in to the madness of his time, clinging with determination to daily prayer, quiet meditation, and scripture reading as the basis for a more human life.

Merton's hermit life offers a model for each one of us. All of us can live more conscious lives of peace and prayer. Any one of us can choose a simple, quiet life and cultivate peace and nonviolence, like Merton. We can take time every day, no matter how busy we are, for peaceful solitude, for quiet meditation, for intercessory prayer. We can let the Holy Spirit of peace settle within us and move through us. If we want to serve the God of peace, Merton seems to say, we better get used to living at peace with ourselves and the God of peace. Otherwise, how can we claim to offer the world an authentic witness for peace? For me, the lesson calls for mindful, peaceful, conscious living, no matter our state in life.

Notice the many key phrases in these beautiful passages: "to live in silence, to think and write, to listen to the wind and to all the voices of the wood, to struggle with a new anguish, to prepare for my exodus to the heavenly country, to love all people, to pray, to offer peace and good sense." These are the goals of anyone who wishes to be a fully conscious, enlightened, and awakened person—that is, a person of peace. "It is a life of peace, silence, purpose and meaning." That's what we all seek but we do not even realize it—peace, silence, purpose, and meaning. "My life is fully human." That one sentence sums up the witness of Thomas Merton. Every one of us is called to be "fully human." Note the connection with God—"only what is authentically human is fit to be offered to God." And so the peacemaker practices "living together with wisdom." Merton shows us one way to fulfill our humanity and invites us to take up that journey without fear or doubt.

In my own life, I swing from periods of intense, active public work—traveling, addressing audiences, leading prayer services and retreats, organizing demonstrations, speaking at rallies—to quiet, solitary work, writing alone in a little handmade house off the grid on a remote mesa in the high desert of New Mexico. Perhaps on that score, I've taken Merton *too* seriously. I literally sought out the same kind of solitude he searched for in New Mexico in the spring and summer of 1968, and I found it on a quiet mountaintop overlooking fifty pristine miles of beautiful New Mexico wilderness in the Galisteo Basin. Merton would have given his eye teeth to live where I live because it is quintessential New Mexico high desert solitude. For ten years now, I've lived alone on this desert mountaintop. I've experienced the sheer joy and ecstasy that Merton extols as the fruit of holy solitude. I know what he's talking about.

The solitude of the New Mexico desert slows one down, restores one's humanity, and puts one in touch with the reality of creation. The silence here is unlike anything else I've experienced. Sometimes at night, a million bright stars shine overhead, and I try to reach up and touch the bright pink Milky Way. The Russian sagebrush and green junipers give the moonscape a mysterious beauty. The smell of the sagebrush, the occasional rainfall, and the spectacular sunsets give my little house an otherworldly context and fill me with consolation. Such peaceful solitude forces you to confront yourself, but it also opens up innumerable blessings for the present moment of peace. I never would have dared such a life without Thomas Merton's strong example.

Merton invites me to experience the holy life of peace as *ordinary*. His daily life in the hermitage was utterly unremarkable, perhaps even boring to the untrained eye, yet it stands in direct contrast to the world of violence and war. In this ordinary life of peace alone in the woods, there is no violence, no kill-ing, no harm, no war. It is a life that noncooperates with every aspect of the culture of violence, so that God's reign of peace and nonviolence might flourish. It is precisely Merton's ordinary daily prayer and nonviolence that seem so extraordinary. As he discovered, there aren't enough hours in the day. He feels more human, more alive, more filled with the Spirit, and those feelings can be hard to come by and sustain amid the culture of violence.

But the difference between Merton's solitude and our own is that his was concentrated solely on God. That's what sets him apart from the millions of others who live alone. Merton returned to the basics so that he could spend all his conscious energy on God—in nature, in prayer, in reading, in peace and quiet. Here's what he writes at the start of his hermit experiment:

> The great joy of the solitary life is not found simply in quiet, in the beauty and peace of nature, in the song of birds or even in the peace of one's own heart. It resides in the awakening and the attuning of the inmost heart to the voice of God—to the inexplicable, quiet definite inner certitude of one's call to obey God, to hear God, to worship God here, now, today in silence and alone. In the realization that this is the whole reason for one's existence.[6]

Two weeks before Merton began to live full-time at the hermitage, he outlined his goal to live in the full conscious awareness of his intimate relationship with God as his beloved Father, as Jesus did, and thus to claim his identity as a beloved son of God. In this way he fulfilled the Beatitude blessing upon peacemakers, that they are the sons and daughters of the God of peace. This for me is the key to the spiritual life of peace and nonviolence. Not only was Merton focused on God, he realized that the only way the solitary life works is through this focus on God. Living in relationship with the God of peace is the whole point of life. We are all called to live in conscious awareness of our intimate relationship with the God of peace, as our beloved father or mother, as God's beloved sons or daughters, and so we dwell in peace with ourselves, with all others, and with creation. Merton continues,

The solitary life, now that I really confront it, is awesome, wonderful, and I see I have no strength of my own for it. Rather I have a deep sense of my own poverty and above all, an awareness of wrongs I have allowed in myself together with this good desire. This is all good. I am glad to be shocked by grace, to wake up in time and see the great seriousness of what I am about to do. . . . I do not see how the really solitary life can tolerate illusion or self-deception. It seems to me that solitude rips off all the masks and all the disguises. It tolerates no lies. Everything but straight and direct affirmation or silence is mocked and judged by the silence of the forest. "Let your speech be yea, yea." The solitary life is to stand in truth; hence the need to pray, the need for theological food, for the Bible, for monastic tradition. The need to be entirely defined by a relationship with and orientation to God my Father; that is to say, a life of sonship in which all that distracts from this relationship is seen as fatuous and absurd. Above all, the work of hope and not the stupid, relaxed, self-pity of acedia. Great need to honor God by personal truth in the personal grace of solitude.[7]

These words show Thomas Merton as a brave spiritual adventurer. He was like a mountain climber, setting off for Everest, clinging to his oxygen tank, determined to reach the top. Notice the discovery and embrace of the brutality of solitude—how it exposes one's poverty and wrongs, rips off all masks and disguises, yet how good it is to be "shocked by grace" and "to wake up," how it requires serious attention to God, and above all, steadfast concentration on "the work of hope." This whole life is a work of peace, hope, and love. In this concentrated nonviolent life, Merton shows us that there is no spiritual life. There is only life, in all its fullness.

Thank God we don't all have to be monks or hermits! We can fall in love, marry, have children, make friends, travel the world, belong to a church, struggle for justice and peace with a local group, enjoy concerts and movies and the arts, serve the needy, and live life to the full in a million ways. But Merton reminds us to go through it all with God—to live deliberately with God, to be conscious of God, to set God first and foremost in our lives. His extraordinary gift of solitude in the woods where he focused on life with the God of peace reminds us to love ourselves and everyone and all creation, but first and foremost, to love God with all our hearts, all our souls, all our mind, and all our strength. This is the work of peace, hope, and love.

A Day in the Life of a Peacemaker

What I wear is pants. What I do is live. How I pray is
    breathe.
Up here in the woods is seen the New Testament.
That is to say, the wind comes through the trees and
    you breathe it.[1]

With those crisp declarations, Merton describes a typical day
in his peacemaking life. On the face of it, Merton's time alone
in the woods was so ordinary, so run-of-the-mill, so boring, no
one would give it a second thought. But that's the mystique of
peace: it appears boring to the mind brainwashed by the culture
of violence, greed, and war. In reality, peace is the fullness of
life. It is the doorway into the Kingdom of God, the presence
of the God of peace.

In "Day of a Stranger," a 1967 essay, Merton takes us through
his daily mindfulness and, in doing so, invites us to live more
mindfully, more consciously, more peacefully in the presence of
the God of peace. I find it his most provocative essay.

I don't know what he means when he says, "Up here in the
woods is seen the New Testament," but I find it infinitely intriguing. I believe him. In his simple, quiet life in the woods, he sees
the fullness of the New Testament. Of course! How could it be
otherwise? The life, death, and resurrection of Jesus; his Sermon
on the Mount teachings; his Pentecost spirit; the height and
breadth and depth and glory of God and God's love; even the
apocalyptic, political implications of gospel nonviolence—after

years of prayer in the monastery, alone in the woods, at a time of cataclysmic turmoil, Merton saw the simplest, mystical vision: the truth of reality. He realized in his being what the early church fathers wrote about so passionately. Like Moses on Sinai, Merton entered the cloud, encountered the God of peace, and received the wisdom of God. That is to say, he breathed in the Holy Spirit and stepped into the New Testament. He realized the faith, hope, love, and peace of the early Christians, something few Christians have done since.

Merton stripped off some of the trappings of religious life and focused on the reality of life in the woods and became, oddly enough, more human, as some of his friends and fellow monks told me. That occurs, first of all, because of his oneness with creation.

> I exist under trees. I walk in the woods out of necessity. I am both a prisoner and an escaped prisoner. I know the birds in fact very well, for there are precise pairs of birds living in the immediate area of my cabin. I share this particular place with them; we form an ecological balance.[2]

Merton goes on to describe waking up at 2:15 a.m. to pray the psalms, sitting in silence, and taking in the fullness of night. "In the formlessness of night and silence, a word pronounces itself: Mercy." Eventually, he walks down to the monastery to fulfill a few errands. There he has duties, obligations; there he is a monk. "When I have accomplished these, I return to the woods where I am nobody." Back at the hermitage, as a nobody, he becomes who he is: the son of God, brother of Christ. He fulfills his vocation, as we now see, though he himself doesn't yet quite see it.

There in the hermitage on a hot summer's day, he sits in the back room where it's cooler, enjoys the silence, reads the psalms. He sweeps, cleans up, writes, prepares a small dinner, and sits again in the cool back room. The birds sing, the breeze blows, and the bells of the monastery ring. It's a lifelong Zen retreat, one perpetual present moment lived in the Holy Spirit of peace.

But periodically, a massive, dark plane carrying nuclear weapons flies low overhead, on its way to Oak Ridge or some other nearby nuclear installation. With the bomb flying overhead, the presence of Death with a capital "D" makes its presence. The world of death in all its fullness notices the peacemaker.

> I have seen the SAC plane, with the bomb in it, fly low over me and I have looked up out of the woods directly at the closed bay of the metal bird with a scientific egg in its breast! A womb easily and mechanically opened! I do not consider this technological mother to be the friend of anything I believe in. However, like everyone else, I live in the shadow of the apocalyptic cherub. I am surveyed by it, impersonally. Its number recognizes my number. Are these numbers preparing at some moment to coincide in the benevolent mind of a computer? This does not concern me, for I live in the woods as a reminder that I am free not to be a number. There is, in fact, a choice.[3]

The image of a nuclear bomber flying directly over the nonviolent hermit and his hermitage of peace helps place the quiet nonviolence of Merton literally in context. It sets his peacemaking life in high relief. Now we begin to understand what this "life without care," as he called it, has to offer. In a world where billions—trillions—of dollars are spent to maintain our nuclear arsenal and prepare for nuclear holocaust, one sane response is a deliberate life of peace, even if that means the solitude of the Kentucky woods. Resistance to the culture of war can take even the form of extreme solitude as Merton and other solitaries show. They keep alive the possibilities of peace and the work of hope, even as all hope seems to disappear.

One of Merton's most ecstatic journal entries comes after an unusual day, January 5, 1965, when he walked through a hidden valley called Edelin's Hallow some ten miles from the monastery to see if the monastery could buy land there in order to build a few more hermitages. There in that valley, Merton was again overcome with peace and consolation. "Never was there such a day," he concluded. And there, too, the SAC plane with its nuclear bomb flew low overhead. It was as if Merton walked through the shadow of death, as if the shadow of the bomb followed his every step, no matter how hard he tried to live in the light of peace and nonviolence.

> I looked up at the clear sky and the tops of the leafless trees shining in the sun and it was a moment of angelic lucidity. I said the Psalms of Tierce with great joy, overflowing joy, as if the land and woods and spring were all praising God through me. Again the sense of angelic transparency of everything: of pure, simple and total light. The word that comes closest to pointing to it is "simple." It was all so simple, but with a simplicity to which one seems to aspire, only seldom to attain it. A simplicity that is and has and says everything just because it is simple.[4]

Then he records an afterthought:

> The SAC planes. I forgot to mention that when I was at the spring after Tierce, when I was about to leave, the huge SAC plane announced its coming and immediately swooped exactly overhead, not more than two or three hundred feet above the hilltops. It was fantastic and sure enough I could see the trap door of the bomb bays. The whole thing was an awesome part of the "simplicity," a sign and an "of course." It had a great deal to do with all the rest of the day.
> During the day, in fact, five SAC planes went over all on the same course, swooping over the hills. Only the first and the last went directly over me, but directly so that I was looking right up at the bomb. This was quite fantastic. Of course, the mere concept of fear was utterly meaningless, out of the question. I felt only an intellectual and moral intuition, a sort of "of course," which seemed to be part of the whole day and of its experience.[5]

The next day, while he was still taking it all in, still another SAC plane swooped down right over the hermitage with its nuclear bomb bay right over the peacemaking hermit. It was "hardly one hundred and fifty feet above the treetops," he wrote.

He went to the woods to turn his back on the Bomb, the culture of war, and in doing so discovered new depths of peace. It almost seems that the Bomb followed him, tracked him down, and sought him out. In his peace, Merton was the real threat, the real power, the stronger force.

Merton's life of prayerful, peaceful mindfulness was not a life of laziness, acedia, or narcissism. It was the fullness of life. While we can easily miss the hard work he put into his writing, the long hours he spent in prayer and scripture study, the endless correspondence and steady stream of visitors, and the constant humiliation he faced from church officials and fellow Catholics, we do catch the hidden detachment that marked the saints and mystics of history. Merton's life was cut off from the culture of violence, but unlike others, it stood as an antidote to the culture of violence.

Merton's peace and nonviolence are so simple that they are easily overlooked. He called this life simply "breathing." But any true spiritual seeker—whether a practicing Buddhist or a nonviolent Christian Bible student—knows that breathing centers us in the present moment and allows the Holy Spirit to move among us. Nothing could be holier, or more meaningful, or more political. Merton was all of these.

In his essay "A Signed Confession of Crimes against the State," published in *The Behavior of Titans*, Merton hints at the political implications of his peaceful life. There he pokes fun at his own contemplative life in the woods, as direct, illegal disobedience to the state and its bomb makers.

Everything that is written, anywhere, or by anybody, is a potential confession of crime against the state. I confess that I am sitting under a pine tree doing absolutely nothing. I have done nothing for one hour and firmly intend to continue to do nothing for an indefinite period. I have taken my shoes off. I confess that I have been listening to a mockingbird. Yes, I admit that is a mockingbird. I hear him singing in those cedars, and I am very sorry. It is probably my fault. He is singing again. This kind of thing goes on all the time. Wherever I am, I find myself the center of reactionary plots like this one.[6]

In our time of "global totalitarianism," as my friend Julian Assange calls it, the state is indeed listening in to everyone—literally everyone on the planet. Every email, every phone call, every text, every message sent by every human being on the planet is saved, stored, and noted. The state now takes note of everything. We are all catalogued and watched, beyond anything Orwell could have imagined. Anyone who dissents from the culture of permanent war and corporate greed finds himself on a secret list. At this rate, sitting under a pine tree, listening to a mockingbird, will soon really be a crime against the state.

The hermit knows there's another side to reality. He has seen the New Testament, breathed in the wind, and entered into the presence of the God of peace. He knows that the God of peace is worth our attention, not the state and its totalitarian ways, not the rat-race culture of the latest sale, not the rush for power and domination.

Life is short. Instead of wasting our days chasing after money, power, or possessions, life is better spent in the present moment, in the presence of the God of peace, getting ready for an eternity of peace in the presence of the God of peace. Life invites us to the work of peace, hope, and love.

How do we do that? For starters, we might sit under a pine tree, listen to the mockingbirds, and breathe in the wind.

The Spiritual Roots of Protest

In November 1964 Merton did something unheard of. He invited the leaders of the U.S. peace movement to come to Gethsemani and make a retreat with him. John Heidbrink, the religious outreach coordinator of the Fellowship of Reconciliation (FOR), an ecumenical peace and nonviolence organization that was heavily involved with Dr. King's growing civil rights movement, had suggested the idea.

Since only men were allowed to make retreats at Gethsemani at that time, only men were invited, but it was a who's who of radical Christian leadership: Fathers Daniel and Philip Berrigan, John Howard Yoder (Mennonite theologian, author of *The Politics of Jesus*), A. J. Muste (leader of the Fellowship of Reconciliation), Jim Forest and Tom Cornell of the Catholic Worker and the Catholic Peace Fellowship, W. H. "Ping" Ferry (of the Santa Barbara Center for the Study of Democratic Institutions), John Oliver Nelson (FOR leader and founder of Kirkridge Retreat Center), John Grady (antiwar activist on the staff of *Jubilee* magazine), Tony Walsh (of the Montreal Catholic Worker), and Elbert Jean (Arkansas civil rights activist). The other participants were Robert Cunnane and Charles Ring, retreat house directors and friends of Phil Berrigan. Martin Luther King Jr. and Bayard Rustin would have joined them, but they were busy preparing King's sudden trip to Norway to accept the Nobel Peace Prize.

By 1967 Merton was writing of repeating the experience, only this time including Dorothy Day, founder of the Catholic Worker; folksinger and activist Joan Baez; church leader Sister

Mary Luke Tobin; and theologian Rosemary Radford Ruether. Just before he died, he did in fact lead two retreats for small groups of religious women, which he later wrote were the best retreats of his life. He intended to host Dr. King, Vincent Harding, and Thich Nhat Hanh for a weeklong retreat in mid-April 1968, but Dr. King's assassination intervened.

Today such retreats happen all the time all over the country and the world, but in 1964 there had never before been such a retreat—a gathering of significant movement leaders to deepen the connection between their political work for peace and the spiritual roots of peace. Certainly, there were parish retreats, men's retreats, women's retreats, and preached retreats, but these days called for reflection on the global crises of war and violence, and the Christian response to such crises. At the time, such a retreat would not have been allowed in any parish in the United States.

It is hard for us to grasp just how influential Merton was, along with Daniel and Philip Berrigan. Up until 1960, no priest in the United States had spoken out against war, violence, or nuclear weapons. The church was completely embedded with the culture of war. There were no alternative voices of nonviolence, except for one: Dorothy Day of the Catholic Worker. Ever since founding the Catholic Worker in 1933, she had denounced U.S. warmaking. She was a lone voice in the wilderness, widely dismissed as a dangerous communist. Of course, now the process of her canonization is under way, but back then she was widely regarded as a dangerous threat. Remember, the first organization of U.S. bishops—long before the U.S. Conference of Catholic Bishops—was formed during World War I for the purpose of supporting the U.S. military. Dorothy Day announced that Jesus wanted us to be peacemakers and love our enemies; no one had ever said that before in U.S. Catholic history.

Then suddenly Merton and the Berrigans start speaking out and acting out for peace—as priests. Why? When I was imprisoned in the 1990s with Philip Berrigan for engaging in a Plowshares disarmament action, I pressed Phil about this. He said there was one simple answer: John Heidbrink. John was trying to get every Christian denomination in the United States to have a small peace group, a voice for peace and nonviolence within their denomination. He succeeded brilliantly—except for the Catholic Church. After serious consideration and discussion, he decided to go and meet the three most famous liberal priests in the country, convert them to peacemaking, and let them inspire a change in the church. So he flew out to Gethsemani and met Merton. Then he flew down to New Orleans and met Phil Berrigan. Then he flew to Syracuse to meet Dan. Merton was also getting to know Dan at the same time, and he was starting to write more publicly about peace. There you can detect an obvious change in his journals. After meeting John and Dan, Merton begins to undergo a conversion to the practice of daily nonviolence. The next thing you know, he's hosting a retreat for the leading peacemakers in the United States, intending to include Dr. King.

I'm reflecting on this event because I think such gatherings are needed today more than ever, and once again, Merton showed the way forward. I wish every monastery and retreat center in the country regularly hosted four-day retreat gatherings where ordinary Christians could gather to share, reflect, and pray over the political work before us (on climate change, drones, global poverty, nuclear weapons, executions, mass incarceration, racism, and so forth) and the spiritual roots for peacemaking. Merton's FOR retreat should inspire us to organize our own retreats or to seek out and attend such retreats. Each participant was inspired and transformed by the Merton retreat.

Initially Merton suggested that they sit around and quietly share together, with no set agenda, but as the day approached, he sent around a sheet with an outline and questions for reflection. He called the weekend "The Spiritual Roots of Protest," and suggested that they spend time together digging at the roots of their nonviolent action, to better understand what they were doing and why. Merton and the others never wrote about the retreat, so this is the only information available, except the excellent recent book about the retreat called *Pursuing the Spiritual Roots of Protest* by Gordon Oyer. I think each one of us can sit with Merton's notes and take his questions to heart as we reflect on our own work for justice and peace:

> We are hoping to reflect together during these days on our common grounds for religious dissent and commitment in

the face of the injustice and disorder of a world in which total war seems at times inevitable, in which few seek any but violent solutions to economic and social problems more critical and more vast than humanity has ever known before. What we are seeking is not the formulation of a program, but a deepening of roots. Roots in the "ground" of all being, in God, through His word. Standing in the presence of His word knowing that we are judged by it. Bringing our inner motives into line with this judgment. Protest: Against whom or what? For what? By what right? How? Why?[1]

"A deepening of roots." What a helpful invitation! Right away, Merton sets the tone of the gathering and calls everyone to slow down, step back, and look deeply within and among themselves for the spiritual basis for the public work for justice and peace in the world of injustice and war. Notice how he then defines what roots we are to deepen—our roots in the Ground of All Being, which is Merton's name for God, and in the Word of God, from the prophets to Jesus who summon us to the work for justice and peace. As we slow down and step back, we reflect on how each one of us stands in the presence of God's prophetic word, and that our lives are judged by this call to work for justice and peace. As mature, mindful Christians, Merton reminds us to reflect deeply on how we are living in relationship with God and God's work as we work for justice and peace. Everything we do for justice and peace in the world comes from that relationship with God and God's word.

Merton continues,

Emphasis has been placed on the question "By what right do we assume that we are called to protest, to judge, and to witness?" If we once (in the past) had a clear right, have we now forfeited it? And are we simply assuming such a "right" or "mandate" by virtue of our insertion in a collective program of one sort or another? An institution? A "movement"?[2]

Merton offers us a new Zen koan for our catastrophic times: By what right do we protest? And his subsequent questions:

Against whom or what? For what? How? Why? That key question, "By what right?" (which he had originally underlined in the handout), stops us in our tracks. The answer is obvious, but on second thought, maybe not so obvious. This is the kind of question that Rilke wrote about, saying it's best not to rush into an answer, but to sit with the question and let it linger within us, even for years, so that one day we live our way into the answer. Merton points to that answer when he reminds us that all our public activity for justice and peace is done within the Ground of All Being, in God, and in God's word.

Everyone who dares to speak out and protest the world's wars needs to sit with Merton's question. In the last few decades, scholars claim nearly two-thirds of the human race has been personally involved in grassroots movements for peace and justice. Over eighty-five nonviolent revolutions have occurred. The Arab Spring and the Occupy movements show the power of public protest to bring about change. Those movements that were nonviolent were the most powerful, the most transformative, the most lasting. But the ongoing violence in the world's protests reveals the need to examine our motivations. Why do we protest? Are we helping to disarm the world or bringing about more harm? Merton and his retreat friends were the first to grapple with these questions, and we all need to do the same.

"We can help one another to a new openness," Merton continues.

> We will think, speak and act as brothers, conscious that one same Spirit works in us, according to the gifts of each, for the manifestation of the justice and truth of God in the world, through Christ. But what do we mean by this? Does it mean only meditation on familiar themes or the awakening of a new eschatological conscience?[3]

An eschatological conscience? What an intriguing way to put our Christian vision for life and the world! Merton goes on to list many topics for discussion—the nature of technological society, its destructive tendencies, and our response; the questions of mass media and communication; the relevance of preaching and worship; the relevance of old, familiar ways of social and political action in these changing times; the relevance and validity of the interior life, asceticism, contemplation, prophetic witness, even intercessory prayer in such times; the meaning of *metanoia*; total personal renewal as a prerequisite for any valid nonviolent action; the role of sacrifice and suffering in redemptive nonviolent protest; and the question of reparatory sacrifice for the sins of racism, war, and so forth.

One could spend the rest of one's life pondering such questions. Merton did just that. So did the Berrigans and the rest of the retreatants. So should we.

Gordon Oyer's book tells about the daily retreat sessions. Merton spoke of monasticism and the monastic approach to these answers, while Daniel Berrigan gave a talk on Teilhard de Chardin's vision of human progress for clues into these questions. They all spent time with Jacques Ellul's work on technology and also reflected on the lone Austrian martyr Franz Jägerstätter, beheaded for refusing to fight for the Nazis and how no one should ever have again to go alone through such a witness for Christ.

But from my perspective it was John Howard Yoder who helped them and the rest of us find new answers. Nowadays, what he said seems so simple and so obvious, but for the time, it was fundamentally new. We protest, he said quietly, because we are followers of the nonviolent Jesus who protested war and empire. Our hope is in Christ. Our protest comes from our discipleship to this nonviolent Jesus, to the risen, peacemaking Christ. We practice a theology and spirituality of the cross, and so we stand up, speak out, protest, and resist. We do so, like Jesus, in a spirit of peace, love, and nonviolence, come what may.

We protest, in other words, because of the nonviolent Jesus. Because the God of peace would have us abolish war, nuclear weapons, extreme poverty, and corporate greed. Because creation is on the brink of destruction. Because we are created to be nonviolent, called to be peacemakers, not warmakers. A few years later, Yoder published *The Politics of Jesus*, the first, and still the best, book on the nonviolence of Jesus and its implications for ourselves, the church, and the world. Since the 1960s, hundreds of theology, scripture, and political books have been written about the nonviolent political action of Jesus, many that have inspired entire new areas of theology, such as liberation and feminist theologies. But at the time, such insights were rare. We see this, for example, in the basic fact that Merton wrote very little about Jesus. On the retreat, Merton's koan led the Christian group to place the focus of their work for justice and peace where it belongs: on the nonviolent Jesus, the God of peace, and the coming of God's reign of peace and nonviolence.

The Merton retreat teaches us the importance of coming together to pray and share with other Christians about the world of war and our responsibility to make peace. As we reflect on their time together, it is important to note what they did *not* talk about: they did not argue about the papacy, denominational differences, salvation, or our individual relationships with God. They discussed the world and our responsibility as Christians. In that sense, it was remarkable that they placed as their guide and model the Austrian martyr Franz Jägerstätter, who had only been discovered a few years earlier by writer Gordon Zahn; Merton and the others took him with utmost seriousness. They knew that not only was Jägerstätter the model Christian peace activist, he was a contemplative and mystic of the highest order. Indeed, Jägerstätter reached a new kind of political mysticism, rarely touched since the days of the early church.

Such peacemaking retreats are needed now more than ever. We need to connect with one another, with all those who struggle for disarmament, justice, and peace. We need to share our concerns, our despair, our hopes, and our lives, discovering together the spiritual roots underlying our work. Together we can seek the God of peace, renew our discipleship to the nonviolent Jesus, build lasting friendships, and discover new depths of faith, hope, and love. Perhaps then we will be better prepared to welcome peace as a gift from God.

The world is stuck in permanent warfare and hovers on the brink of destruction. When Merton called other Christian peacemakers to reflect and pray together, he strengthened the growing movement of gospel nonviolence. That's what happens whenever we gather to reflect, pray, and share our concerns over the predicament of the world: we are reenergized to follow the nonviolent Jesus and go forth as protesters and peacemakers to build up the growing global grassroots movements of nonviolence.

A personal note: Over the years I came to know and befriend many of the retreat participants—Dan and Phil Berrigan, Jim Forest and Tom Cornell, John Grady and Ping Ferry, and John Howard Yoder. Then, in the 1990s, when I became executive director of the Fellowship of Reconciliation, the peace group that proposed and sponsored Merton's peace retreat, I came to know the great John Heidbrink. John and I corresponded and spoke periodically on the phone.

Shortly before he died, he sent me an extraordinary gift: a copy of *A Thomas Merton Reader*, signed by everyone at this famous Gethsemani peace retreat. The week before the FOR retreat, in November 1964, John Heidbrink fell ill and was admitted to a Nyack, New York, hospital, near FOR headquarters. As the gathering concluded, Merton asked everyone to sign the book as a gift. "To John—from Tom Merton." "To John with love—from Dan Berrigan." "To John—from A. J. Muste." And so forth.

John Heidbrink wanted me to have it, and sent it on as a gift. I always felt that the good seeds sown by Merton, the Berrigans, and these other peacemakers took root in my own life. In particular, this peacemaking retreat inspired me to connect with other like-minded friends in the work for peace. The retreat lives on in my own life and among my friends, with that signed book as a living reminder.

"The encounter has loomed large in the imaginations of many religious peace advocates," Gordon Oyer writes. "Its intent of gathering in mutual respect to consult one another regarding the spiritual implications of protesting the powers of domination supplies us with a profound, iconic image. It reminds us of a fundamental call to dig deeply and tap into spiritual roots that will set our priorities, sustain our vision, and navigate our pilgrimage as we give voice to hopes and aspirations that coax humanity closer to its created intent."[4]

The Work of Hope

Summing up his new hermitage experiment with solitude, Merton writes that he can now get on with the great task at hand—"the work of hope."

What a provocative phrase! I find it helpful because, between you and me, I have always struggled with hope. Unfortunately, by nature, I am a pessimist. This naturally has to do with my childhood upbringing, the ordeals I have endured, and my take on the world. But long ago I was taught the difference between optimism and hope. Hope, for me, takes the long-haul view—I mean the *really* long-haul view—of salvation history, the story of the universe, the eschaton, that day in the Kingdom of God when every human being will be raised and restored together in the love of Christ and we will live together in peace happily ever after. For most, that is a dream, but for me, it's a matter of faith. And it comes at a great price, with tremendous political implications for the here-and-now world of war and injustice. We have to give our lives now for suffering humanity if we believe such a long-haul view. And entering that nonviolent struggle for justice can only lead to the unearned suffering love of the cross. So for me, the life of hope is hard work.

In light of Merton's phrase, we might consider our own lives, our efforts for justice and peace, and how we live in the world within that framework of hope. How do our lives and work generate hope for ourselves, humanity, and creation? This question can help us dig deeper Merton roots into our spiritual lives.

The first thing I hear in Merton's life assessment is the fundamental recognition that we do not have any hope. We live in a world of despair, a world of no hope whatsoever. Few like to put it so baldly, but I believe, with Merton, that most of us walk around in a state of functional despair. That we might not know it is part of the disease.

There in his house in the woods, Merton knew that most people have flat-out given up. He could read the signs of the times, the writing on the wall. He could see what lay in store—more and more violence, warfare, nuclear war, poverty, injustice, environmental destruction. If we dare look long and hard at reality without blinking, we realize that we are well beyond hope, that at best we practice a false hope, a cheap hope. Merton teaches us that the first step on the road to hope is to recognize our global reality of violence, death, and destruction, and the consequential despair that has seeped into each of us in varying degrees.

What can any one person do in the face of systemic injustice, endless war, nuclear weapons, starvation, and catastrophic climate change? Can anything really be done? Is it even worth trying to make a difference? If indeed the God of peace is so non-violent that God gives humanity the freedom to choose between life or death, and therefore remains powerless to intervene even against our worst violence, aren't people of goodwill likewise powerless and helpless in the face of systemic evil? Shouldn't we throw up our hands, give in to despair, and resign ourselves to hopeless helplessness?

No, Merton insists. That is not the Christian way. Christians are people of hope. We are disciples of the nonviolent Jesus, who carried on despite all odds, in the face of strenuous opposition, even unto betrayal, denial, torture, and execution. We are people of faith who believe in the living God of peace. We know that with the God of peace all things are possible. We understand that if we have faith the size of a mustard seed, we can move mountains; that is, with faith, hope, and active love, together we can do the impossible and end slavery, segregation, and apartheid—even peacefully bring down the Berlin Wall. We trust in the resurrection. We seek the Kingdom of God, pray for its coming, welcome it wholeheartedly, and resist all the other kingdoms and allegiances and false gods. We practice hope. We can't afford the bourgeois luxury of despair. So we struggle for hope, we work for it, we go forward in hope and pay the cost of hope in a time of total despair.

Hope is the ordinary work of the Christian.

But what is "the work of hope"? That's a good question to sit with. The work of hope begins in our own hearts and lives as we take care of ourselves, make peace with ourselves and God, and create a peaceful future for ourselves. It means building peaceful relationships with one another, in the workplace, in our local communities and cities, and in our shared religious practice—the Eucharist, the sacraments, scripture reading, and so forth.

For Merton, however, the work of hope is far more than getting a good job, making money, or achieving power, honor, and prestige. For Merton, the work of hope does not allow any trace of selfishness or narcissism. The work of hope means engaging the world, joining the grassroots movements for disarmament and justice, welcoming the Kingdom of God, and giving our lives for humanity.

Merton wrote many powerful essays that could be understood within the context of this work. Let me reflect on just one: "Peace and Protest." There he writes,

> I see war as an avoidable tragedy and I believe that the problem of solving international conflict without massive violence has become the number-one problem of our time. The task of humanity and of the Church is to end all wars, to provide a satisfactory [nonviolent] international power to police the world and subdue violence while conflicts are settled by reason and negotiation. Therefore the entire human race has a most serious obligation to face this problem and to do something about it. Each one of us has to resist an ingrained tendency to violence and destructive thinking. Every time we renounce reason and patience in order to solve a conflict by violence, we are side-stepping this great obligation and putting it off. How long can we continue to do this? Our time is limited, and we are not taking advantage of our opportunities.
>
> The human race today is like an alcoholic who knows

that drink will destroy him and yet always has "good reasons" why he must continue drinking. Such is humanity in its fatal addiction to war. Humanity is not really capable of seeing a constructive alternative to war.

If this task of building a peaceful world is the most important task of our time, it is also the most difficult. It will, in fact, require far more discipline, more sacrifice, more planning, more thought, more cooperation and more heroism than war ever demanded.

The task of ending war is in fact the greatest challenge to human courage and intelligence. Can we meet this challenge? Do we have the moral strength and the faith that are required? Sometimes the prospect seems almost hopeless, for humanity is more addicted to violence now than ever before, and we are today spending more for war alone than we spent for everything, war included, thirty years ago. We also live in a crisis of faith in which to most "God is dead" and even some Christians no longer accept Christ except as a symbol.[1]

Perhaps we roll our eyes or turn the page as Merton—and I—go on and on about the duty to end war and violence. Is this too boring, repetitive, uninteresting? Do we disengage at the first sound of such dreamy political rhetoric? Could that boredom from war talk be a deep sign of our despair?

I don't know how to write or speak about this in an interesting way. I think Merton, the writing genius, tried every avenue possible through his writing to sound the alarm. But the wake-up call rings throughout all his writing—in his autobiography, his journals, his letters, his poems, his essays, and his theology. I want us to take to heart what Thomas Merton is saying so urgently and creatively, after decades of silence, meditation, scripture study, liturgy, and prayer: that God is a God of peace and wants us to abolish war once and for all. But that is impossible, we say to ourselves. Nothing can be done; even Merton was helpless to advance such a noble cause.

I remember talking about this with one of the monks of Gethsemani, a close friend of Merton, the late Father Matthew

Kelty. I had just addressed the community, and he said to me about my life work for peace, "Well, John, it's a totally hopeless cause, but such a good one."

I suppose I disagree. With Merton, I have to disagree. This is what hope looks like—hope is the work and struggle for the Kingdom of God in a kingdom of violence and war. There is nothing more hopeful. It can appear as pure idealism or downright craziness, but for Merton, this is the heart of the spiritual life. It's why he writes that everything in his life came together in the hermitage so that he can get down to the hard "work of hope."

So what do we do? Merton writes,

> What is needed is a constructive dissent that recalls people to their senses, makes them think deeply, plants in them a seed of change and awakens in them the profound need for truth, reason and peace which is implanted in humanity's nature. Such dissent implies belief in openness of mind and in the possibility of mature exchange of ideas. . . . The way to silence error is by truth, not by violence. But we will always prefer violence to truth if our imaginations are at every moment overstimulated by frenzied and dangerous fantasies. Therefore one of the most important tasks of the moment is to recognize the great problem of the mental climate in which we live. Our minds are filled with images which call for violence and erratic reactions. We can hardly recover our senses long enough to think calmly and make reasoned commitments.
>
> All protest against war and all witness for peace should in some way or other strive to overcome the desperation and hopelessness with which humanity now, in fact, regards all existing peacemaking machinery as futile and beyond redemption.[2]

For Merton, the work of hope employs every nonviolent means for "constructive dissent" to help humanity reclaim the imagination for peace and then move into action. We struggle to lift up the vision of a new world without war and injustice, and show people that this vision is worth our pursuit, that it is not an impossible ideal but an achievable, realizable, doable goal.

We struggle to help reawaken the human imagination and thus the human conscience, so that together we might take concrete steps to institutionalize, nationalize, and globalize nonviolence.

Merton's work of hope invites every living human being to learn and adopt the wisdom and methodologies of nonviolence to lay the groundwork for a future day in coming generations when we formally abolish warfare as a way to resolve conflict, when we finally dismantle our weapons of mass destruction and use those infinite resources to end hunger, poverty, disease, and environmental destruction. Someday in the future, we will institutionalize nonviolent conflict resolution between the nations, and educate every human being on the planet in the way of nonviolence. We want to make nonviolence normative, at every level for everyone—individually, communally, nationally, and globally. This is the work of a lifetime, the work of generations, the work that must go on till the end of time. It is the work of the spiritual life.

The work of hope, according to Merton, requires resisting our own violence and practicing nonviolence as best we can, then communicating to others the many nonviolent alternatives available. We do that by writing, teaching, advocating, building movements, taking public action, and offering a faithful witness. In the last decade of his own life, Merton actively supported several movements and organizations working for peace and justice, and he supported activists around the world as best he could. We can all do our part, he seems to say, even if we live alone in the woods, and he was determined to do his. We can each support the myriad campaigns and movements of nonviolence that are sweeping through the world at this very moment. As we stay involved in these movements for peace and justice, and do our little bit, we help generate hope for ourselves and the world, even though we may not know it or live to see any tangible results. We keep going with the work of hope—living the life of peace, advocating peace, supporting the grassroots movements, and keeping alive the vision of God's reign of peace on earth. This is the work of hope.

"If you want to be hopeful," Daniel Berrigan once said, "you have to do hopeful things." I think the work of hope calls each one of us, in such a time, to become an activist for justice and peace, in whatever form that might take. If we sit back and do nothing, we have given in to despair. We reject the hope of Christ and the coming of the Kingdom of God. Merton did not sit back and do nothing. He was actively engaged with the world, undertaking the work of hope for the church and the world. We can do the same. Each one of us is needed, and each one of us can make a difference.

The problem with this work to end war and the causes of war is that we soon realize how futile this effort appears and can easily fall into greater despair than when we started. We want tangible, immediate, visible results. We want to end the Vietnam War now, or the Nicaraguan war, or the Iraq war, or the Afghanistan war, or world hunger, or catastrophic climate change. For some, the harder you work for the hope of disarmament and justice, the more hopeless things appear.

Merton announced that this was a grave temptation, and not the truth. He said it betrayed a lack of faith in God and a deep misunderstanding of the power of active nonviolence, the power that God has given us to organize love and truth as a methodology for social change. Merton knew well this temptation and wrote famously in 1965 to his friend Jim Forest of the Catholic Peace Fellowship to be on his guard about where he placed his hope; otherwise, he would soon give up.

> Do not depend on the hope of results. When you are doing the sort of work you have taken on, essentially an apostolic work, you may have to face the fact that your work will be apparently worthless and even achieve no result at all, if not perhaps results opposite to what you expect. As you get used to this idea you start more and more to concentrate not on the results but on the value, the rightness, the truth of the work itself. . . .
>
> All that you and I can ever hope for in terms of visible results is that we will have perhaps contributed something to a clarification of Christian truth in this society, and as a result a few people may have got straight about some things and opened up to the grace of God and made some sense out of their lives, helping a few more to do the same.

As for the big results, these are not in your hands or mine, but they can suddenly happen, and we can share in them: but there is no point in building our lives on this personal satisfaction, which may be denied us and which after all is not that important.

So the next step in the process is for you to see that your own thinking about what you are doing is crucially important. . . . All the good that you will do will come not from you but from the fact that you have allowed yourself, in the obedience of faith, to be used by God's love. Think of this more and gradually you will be free from the need to prove yourself and you can be more open to the power that will work through you without your knowing it. If you can get free from the domination of causes and just serve Christ's truth, you will be able to do more and will be less crushed by the inevitable disappointments.

The real hope, then, is not in something we think we can do but in God who is making something good out of it in some way we cannot see. If we can do God's will, we will be helping in this process. But we will not necessarily know all about it beforehand.[3]

Do the good because it's good, Merton advises. Do what's right because it's right. Work for the abolition of war and seek God's reign of peace because this is the greatest cause in history, because this is what Jesus did, this is what God requires, this gives ultimate meaning to our lives. Place your hope then in God, and learn that the outcome is in better hands than ours; it's in God's hands. This lifelong struggle, undertaken in love, is the victory.

This is an ancient spiritual teaching. Instead of worrying about results, we give our lives for justice and peace in pursuit of God's reign and trust that God will use our efforts for God's greater purpose. We love everyone, resist empire, and surrender our lives to God and God's work. We try to mobilize people through creative nonviolence, as Gandhi and King did, into a new grass-roots movement for disarmament, justice, and stewardship of the earth. As we do, we change the world, beginning with our little corner of it. And know that God is the one doing it. Our hope is in God, and so we embark on this journey with others to undertake the impossible. We're like the abolitionists of old who pursued the impossible dream of a world without slavery. Most of them never lived to see their dream realized, but it would never have happened without their persistent lifelong efforts.

That's what Merton is calling us to. Avoid the push for immediate results, remain faithful to the work of hope, let your life bear good fruit in God's own time. Along the way, concentrate on the love of others and the blessings of creation and life. We might enjoy small victories along the way, but even the defeats can be understood within the long-haul victory to come. We take heart knowing that we played our part in God's salvific work through history to bring a more just, peaceful world.

In the 1950s Merton began corresponding with the Polish writer Czeslaw Milosz, who suffered tremendously under communist rule and found life hard to bear and hope an impossible dream. His essays and poems dealt with life under the iron rule of the state. Long before anyone else in the West, Merton discovered in Milosz one of the great voices of the century. Milosz would later move to the United States, meet with Merton on two occasions, teach at the University of California–Berkeley, and eventually receive the Nobel Prize for literature. Their correspondence, published in 1996 as *Striving towards Being*, delves deep into the question of hope and despair.

"The only thing that is to be regretted without qualification is for a man to adapt perfectly to totalitarian society," Merton wrote on September 12, 1959. "Then he is indeed beyond hope." He continued,

> Hence we should all be sick in some way. We should all feel near to despair in some sense because this semi-despair is the normal form taken by hope in a time like ours. Hope without any sensible or tangible evidence on which to rest. Hope in spite of the sickness that fills us. Hope married to a firm refusal to accept any palliatives or anything that cheats hope by pretending to relieve apparent despair. And I would add that hope must mean acceptance of limitations and imperfections and the deceitfulness of a nature that has been wounded and cheated of love and security: this too

we all feel and suffer. Thus we cannot enjoy the luxury of a hope based on our own integrity, our own honesty, our own purity of heart.[4]

For Merton, hope often takes the form of despair. That is a profound truth. Those who dare struggle for hope learn to look deeply into the unspeakable darkness of systemic violence, permanent war, institutionalized injustice, and catastrophic climate change—and still they choose to go on, working for disarmament and positive social change. This is the work of hope in the life of the nonviolent Jesus. Even unto torture and execution, he manifests hope in God and humanity, and keeps on practicing hope. He trusts that his life will bear good fruit, that even his friends will regroup and carry on his work, that death does not get the last word.

In the end, for the Christian who dares to engage in the work of hope, everything boils down to resurrection. Do you believe in the resurrection of Jesus or not? Do you believe in your own resurrection or not? If not, then there is no hope and we are all the greatest of fools. If so, then the victory has already occurred, life has triumphed over death, and eventually the reign of peace will be realized here on earth.

On February 28, 1959, Merton wrote to Milosz,

Life is on our side. The silence and the Cross of which we know are forces that cannot be defeated. In silence and suffering, in the heartbreaking effort to be honest in the midst of dishonesty (most of all our *own* dishonesty), in all these is victory. It is Christ in us who drives us through darkness to a light of which we have no conception and which can only be found by passing through apparent despair. Everything has to be tested. All relationships have to be tried. All loyalties have to pass through fire. Much has to be lost. Much in us has to be killed, even much that is best in us. But Victory is certain. The Resurrection is the only light.[5]

Life is on our side! The Resurrection is the only light! Because death does not win out, because we are all headed to a surprising resurrection, we go forward on the path of peace and nonviolence. Like Merton, we live in peace, say our prayers, help others as best we can, and carry on the work of hope. We keep our eyes on the risen Christ, trust in the God of peace, and lift up a seemingly impossible vision.

We must become practitioners of resurrection. Then we will be people of authentic hope.

15

Thich Nhat Hanh Is My Brother

In 1966 the Fellowship of Reconciliation brought to the United States from Vietnam one of the leading Vietnamese voices for peace, Thich Nhat Hanh, a young Buddhist monk, poet, author, and intellectual. John Heidbrink brought him to Gethsemani where Nhat Hanh met and befriended Merton. He also brought Nhat Hanh to Syracuse to spend time with Daniel Berrigan and to Chicago to meet Martin Luther King Jr., who subsequently nominated Thich Nhat Hanh for the Nobel Peace Prize.

Because Nhat Hanh's speaking tour and meetings, just as the U.S. war on Vietnam was accelerating, were so high profile, his planned return home was immensely dangerous. Hundreds of his monk friends were killed during the war, and there was a high probability that he would be immediately arrested and imprisoned, and probably tortured and executed. Eventually, he decided not to return home. Brokenhearted over his exile, he settled in Paris, later started a monastic community near Bordeaux called Plum Village, and founded a religious order, the Order of Inter-Being. These days, in his late eighties, he still lives in France. He has published over one hundred books on peaceful living, and each year he tours the world giving talks on mindfulness, drawing hundreds of thousands to hear him. In the United States his appearances draw up to ten thousand people. His message is a simple call to mindfulness—that we practice living in the present moment, concentrate on our breath, become as conscious and aware as possible, and live as mindfully as possible in our day-to-day lives, even through ordinary tasks like eating, doing the dishes, and cleaning the house. Today, he is perhaps the leading teacher of peace in the world, and his teachings on mindfulness continue to help millions.

As did Dan Berrigan, Dr. King, and John Heidbrink, Merton instantly recognized that the small Vietnamese monk with the quiet voice, childlike face, and brown robes was a spiritual giant. Like the others, Merton could even foresee his global leadership. But it's hard for us to grasp the politically charged nature of their embrace. Merton, Daniel Berrigan, and Dr. King each embraced Nhat Hanh as a spiritual leader and a peacemaker par excellence, and became intimate friends with him—just as the United States was radically escalating its war on Vietnam. In other words, they were publicly siding with the enemy.

Few Americans understood what was happening in Vietnam, except that many young men were suddenly being called up and shipped off. Fewer still protested it; most everyone went along with the Pentagon propaganda about the communist threat and the need to bomb, napalm, and kill the Vietnamese to protect "our American way of life." Merton, Dan, and Dr. King found a reasonable human voice for peace and spiritual enlightenment in one of our enemies. Nothing could be more radical. This was "love for one's enemies," the hallmark of the Sermon on the Mount, at its best. What touches me is that they each did this not just as an act of political solidarity as a means to end the war, which was very helpful; they actually loved Nhat Hanh.

In response to the real possibility that Nhat Hanh would be killed if he returned, Merton issued a public plea asking people of goodwill everywhere to call for his protection. They hoped Merton's statement and other forms of support would draw international publicity to Nhat Hanh, and thus ensure his protection. Merton's essay "Nhat Hanh Is My Brother," written immediately after his visit, calls for action in solidarity with Nhat Hanh. But it also tells us something about Merton himself, what Merton learned from this peacemaking genius, and how we might all live in solidarity with one another, especially those targeted by our nation's bombs, napalm, drones, and nuclear weapons. He writes,

Thich Nhat Hanh is more my brother than many who are nearer to me by race and nationality, because he and I see things exactly the same way. He and I deplore the war that is ravaging his country. We deplore it for exactly the same reasons: human reasons, reasons of sanity, justice and love. We deplore the needless destruction, the fantastic and callous ravaging of human life, the rape of the culture and spirit of an exhausted people. It is surely evident that this carnage serves no purpose that can be discerned and indeed contradicts the alleged intentions of the mighty nation that has constituted itself "the defender" of the people it is destroying.

We are both monks, and we have lived the monastic life about the same number of years. We are both poets, both existentialists. I have far more in common with Nhat Hanh that I have with many Americans and I do not hesitate to say it. It is vitally important that such bonds be admitted. They are the bonds of a new solidarity and a new brotherhood which is beginning to be evident on all continents and which cuts across all political, religious and cultural lines to unite young men and women in every country in something that is more concrete than an ideal and more alive than a program.

Do what you can for him. If I mean something to you, then let me put it this way: do for Nhat Hanh whatever you would do for me if I were in his position. In many ways I wish I were.[1]

Merton speaks of "a new solidarity and a new brotherhood which is just beginning." Fifty years later, I think this has come true. One will not read about it in the *New York Times* or hear about it on Fox News, but through the various peace movements, many Americans of goodwill have quietly befriended people on the other side of the global divide. Such friendships have the power to transform not only the lives of those involved but entire communities and populations. They can literally save us. I think of my friend Janice who made many peace and solidarity trips to the Soviet Union during the 1970s and 1980s, and became close friends with many Russians. I think of so many friends who developed lifelong intimate relationships with people in Nicaragua, El Salvador, and Guatemala, at the height of the U.S. wars there. I think of so many friends who have given their lives to Haiti, first of all because of the friendships that were established. I myself have good friends in Northern Ireland, El Salvador, Mexico, Haiti, Palestine, the Philippines, South Africa, and Afghanistan. This type of peacemaking, this concrete way to fulfill the call of the Sermon on the Mount, was modeled by Merton, Daniel Berrigan, and Dr. King as they reached out to Thich Nhat Hanh.

Merton's lectures to the scholastics and Sunday afternoon optional talks to the community were recorded over the last eight years or so of his life. By chance, I once listened to the tape recorded just after Thich Nhat Hanh's visit, and I remember him discussing with the scholastics his conversation with Nhat Hanh. He told Merton that when he entered the Buddhist monastery as a teenager they spent the first two years, before any instruction about sitting and quiet meditation, "learning how to close doors." Merton said, "That's what we need around here!" and all the scholastics laughed. Merton reflected on the importance of mindfulness, especially for monastic life. The Buddhist monastery knew that they had to train the young monks to be as mindful as possible, and that meant concentrating first of all on the small details of ordinary living—getting dressed in the morning, brushing your teeth, eating your food, walking down the hall, listening to others, looking at the landscape, attending to your breath, drinking your tea, and closing a door.

Most of us rush through our day-to-day lives. That is not peaceful living. A peacemaker learns to slow down, concentrate on the present moment, breathe in and out, be attentive to whatever presents itself, and do every ordinary deed with as much mindful peaceableness as possible. That means that we are peaceful, mindful, with ourselves, and with others as we drive, work, eat, and walk. We noncooperate with the rush of mindlessness, with the culture of violence. We try to live centered in the present moment of peace, in the Holy Spirit of peace, and in the presence of the God of peace, so that every moment, every word, every act is a sacrament, charged with grace. Merton continues,

Nhat Hanh is a free man who has acted as a free man in favor of his brothers and sisters and [is] moved by the spiritual dynamic of a tradition of religious compassion. He has come among us as many others have, bearing witness to the spirit of Zen. More than any other, he has shown us that Zen is not an esoteric and world-denying cult of inner illumination, but that it has [a] rare and unique sense of responsibility in the modern world. Wherever he goes he will walk in the strength of his spirit and in the solitude of the Zen monk who sees beyond life and death.[2]

Here Merton points to the teachings and lessons that he learned from Nhat Hanh, long before the rest of the world, and urges us to consider the benefits of Zen Buddhist practice, the way of mindfulness that sees beyond life and death to live in the eternal now. I think Merton's encounter with Nhat Hanh had a profound impact on Merton's life, fanning his desire to get to Asia, a dream that came true and led to his historic meetings with the Dalai Lama. It's inspiring, too, to fantasize about what good fruit would have come from Merton's planned weeklong retreat with Dr. King and Thich Nhat Hanh, tentatively planned for mid-April 1968, and ultimately quashed because of Dr. King's assassination.

On his way to Asia, when Merton stopped in Santa Barbara and joined a conference of intellectuals and visionaries, he had a good conversation with Benedictine monk and writer David Steindl-Rast. Years later Br. David wrote that Merton told him, in effect, that the only way to survive Catholicism—with its emphasis on rules, hierarchy, power structure, and obligations (and its lack of emphasis on the Sermon on the Mount, and the implications of the cross and resurrection of Jesus)—is to practice Zen Buddhism, the way of mindfulness. "I intend to become a very good Buddhist," Merton said. By that he did not mean he was leaving the Catholic Church; rather, he was learning the wisdom of Zen to live in the present moment with Christ in conscious mindfulness to fulfill his vocation as a Catholic monk.

Given the total violence of the world, catastrophic climate change, and the ongoing crises of the church, I think Merton's way forward is helpful for all serious Catholics, Christians, and seekers. We all need to learn from Thich Nhat Hanh how to become more conscious, more aware, more mindful. Indeed, one could even define nonviolence as full awareness. Gandhi once called nonviolence "the highest level of conscious living."

Mindfulness does not mean walking on eggshells and becoming zombies or living in a dream state. Quite the opposite. Mindfulness and nonviolence call us to live in the presence of the God of peace, fully alive, alert, eyes wide open, attentive, aware of the present moment, conscious of what lies before us right now, attuned to our breathing, our thoughts, our hopes. Mindful living can open the door to the life of peace, to the Kingdom of God that is here at hand.

Merton learned the lesson from his "enemy" (someone from a country labeled as an enemy of the United States, who became his friend and teacher. That's one reason we should take Jesus at his word and do what he says, including love our enemies, because they can show us the way forward into the Kingdom of God.

A personal note: Years ago, in the 1990s, when I served as executive director of the Fellowship of Reconciliation, I spent a day with Thich Nhat Hanh. I had read his books for years and heard him speak in 1990 in Berkeley, but that first day together, on a farm in Vermont, we became friends. We have visited on several occasions since, and like Merton, Dan Berrigan, and thousands of others, I, too, love him as a friend and teacher. I have spent time with him in his community of Plum Village in France, and I know firsthand the profound beauty and witness of his peacemaking life and nonviolence. He embodies the way of mindfulness as the way of peace, and he has helped me greatly on my own personal journey to peace. He continues to practice to this day, inviting the rest of us to do the same. Like Merton, I, too, say, "Nhat Hanh is my brother." Happily, that statement is becoming true for many Christians.

16

Not Survival, but Prophecy

In February 1968, when French monk and theologian Jean Leclercq wrote to Merton to tell him about the international gathering of monastic leaders that he was organizing for later in the year in Bangkok and invited Merton to attend, Merton wrote back with great interest and announced his message: "The vocation of the monk in the modern world is not survival but prophecy."[1]

That to my mind is one of Merton's great bombshells.

I think it should be broadened: "The vocation of the Christian is not survival but prophecy. The purpose of monasticism and any religious order is not survival but prophecy." And, "The purpose of the church is not survival but prophecy."

That changes everything.

This profound insight and prophetic statement is needed today more than ever because today, as in Merton's day, prophetic individuals, prophetic communities, and prophetic institutions are usually widely misunderstood and universally condemned from those on high. There is very little understanding of the role of the prophetic voice within the church. But Judaism without the prophets is lost. Likewise, Christianity without its prophets is dead. Indeed, one could make the case that in the Sermon on the Mount, Jesus is clearly forming his disciples to become like the prophets of old. When you are persecuted for working for justice and for following me, rejoice and be glad, he says, because then you are like Jeremiah, Isaiah, and Daniel; now you have joined the ranks of Gandhi, Dorothy Day, and Dr. King. Perhaps then to be a Christian is to be a prophet.

Merton's pronouncement to Jean LeClercq should be pondered far and wide. The grave problem with any institution that survives for fifty years—much less two thousand years—is that it gets staid and stymied. It becomes comfortable and no longer rocks the boat. The Catholic Church was founded on the life of the greatest prophet of human history, Jesus of Nazareth. During the first three centuries, there was no survival to be had if you were a follower of the Way. You pledged allegiance to Christ, which meant you refused to swear an oath to Caesar, which meant you were beheaded later that afternoon. But then the church made peace with the empire; soon it modeled itself on the empire. It created leaders to be like little emperors over their own little empires. Over the centuries, these little emperors formed their own armies and waged holy wars to kill millions of heathens. By the twentieth century, it had become so ossified that the administrators seemed to feel they were gods, they were infallible, that the institution itself was the whole point of existence. They forgot, as Daniel Berrigan writes, that the raft is not the shore.

In other words, the whole point of the church was survival.

Once that becomes the goal—instead of following Jesus the prophet, accompanying him to the cross and the resurrection, and announcing the Kingdom of God—we lose our way. We're lost.

It's no wonder then that the German bishops of the 1930s acquiesced to the rise of National Socialism; that white South African bishops supported apartheid; that so many Latin American bishops sided with the dictators, juntas, and death squads; that so many U.S. bishops support U.S. wars and nuclear weapons; that the priestly pedophilia scandal should be covered up at all costs.

The purpose of the church is not prophecy, but survival.

I learned in my training to become a priest that the point at best was to serve as a pastor. We were told deliberately not to rock the boat of church or state. Later I learned that any prospective bishop has to agree, before he would ever be named as bishop, not to speak out on anything, but to toe every line that comes down from on high. Otherwise, they won't even be considered for the office by those who make the decisions.

Is Thomas Merton right? If he is, what does that mean today for monasticism, religious life, and the church?

I think he is right, and it means that every Christian institution, and every Christian, has to rediscover its prophetic calling. We are not only a pastoral people, we are a prophetic people.

I have witnessed the best example of this in recent history. In the mid-1980s at the height of the war, I lived for a while in El Salvador under the tutelage of the Jesuits at their university in downtown San Salvador. Six of these Jesuits, including Ignacio Ellacuría, the university president, were brutally assassinated in 1989. Ellacuría had helped write the pastoral letters of Archbishop Oscar Romero, who was assassinated while saying Mass on March 24, 1980. Almost overnight, as everyone now knows, Romero had become the world's leading prophet, denouncing the death squads and injustices within El Salvador, calling for peace, justice, and the Kingdom of God. Ellacuría and the Jesuits at the university took Romero deadly seriously, and applied his prophetic ministry to the entire Jesuit University.

For the first time in modern history, an entire Christian institution, not just a local parish, set as its primary goal promoting the reign of God. That meant, as Ellacuría told me, that every office, class, teacher, and student had to work toward ending the war and injustices within El Salvador. For example, the chair of the department of engineering told me that he was teaching his students how to rebuild the destroyed bridges and houses within the country. The psychology department was educating students to help survivors deal with posttraumatic stress disorder. The theology department was exploring liberation theology and reflecting on God's preference for the poor and the oppressed. The university printing press published the leading tracts on revolutionary change, what a more democratic society might look like, and how to construct civil society after years of military rule. I spent time in that press and saw their booklets. I couldn't believe what I was reading. There is simply nothing like it in the United States, even with all our universities and colleges. It would be as if Berkeley or Harvard or Princeton announced that the sole purpose of the university was to work for abolishing nuclear weapons.

When twenty-eight soldiers, nineteen of them trained in Georgia at the notorious School of the Americas, raided the Jesuit house above the Romero Center for Theology on November 16, 1989, and killed every priest who was at home, they also destroyed the library, the books, the computers, and their records. Literally the first shot fired was at a large photograph of Romero in the entranceway. As the soldiers burst through the door, one of them shot at Romero's heart. It was as if he was trying to kill Romero, who had been dead already for nine years. These soldiers—with the backing of the Salvadoran president, government, and U.S. government—were trying to stop the prophetic ministry of the university by killing the prophets. Those Salvadoran government officials and death squad leaders felt the pinch of truth that the Jesuit University announced consistently to the nation and to the world. Since the government only knew violence, it responded with violence.

The assassination of the university president and the other leaders of the nation's largest Catholic university should have logically meant the death of the university. They were already financially strapped. It was wartime, and they lived in one of the poorest countries of the world. They had no money. Their very survival was in jeopardy.

But as the early church knew, the blood of the martyrs is the seed of liberty. The death of the Jesuits helped lead to the end of the war within six months. It also led the U.S. Congress to give some $10 million in aid to the Jesuit University, a huge gift that put the institution back on its feet. Oddly enough, the prophetic stand guaranteed the university's survival.

In his time, Merton understood all of this. He knew that the greatest need in the world right now was the announcement of truth. We may not become prophets as individuals, but we can certainly all become together a prophetic people, whether in our parish community, Catholic school, or religious order. He believed that every monastery should be a prophetic community that shares the truth of God, the Word of God, with its local community and nation, if not the world. He also believed that the institutional church should be the leading prophetic voice to the nations, announcing the coming of the Kingdom of God in all its nonviolence, and therefore denouncing in no uncertain terms every nation's violence and injustice. This again is the work of hope, the ministry of the church.

Merton taught that with the resurrection of Jesus, our survival is guaranteed. That means individually and collectively as followers of Jesus. If anything, the institutional church should head deliberately toward the cross, to share in the martyrdom of Jesus, by confronting empire and the forces of death, risking its own existence, and demonstrating to others its trust in God and practice of gospel nonviolence. Every local parish should likewise be a prophetic voice to its local community, calling people to their true selves, speaking out for disarmament and justice, denouncing their nation's wars and injustices, and leading people back to God and the Word of God. He hoped that his own monastery and every monastery would be a prophetic voice in the wilderness, calling us back to the God of peace, modeling the life of peace for one and all.

What does this insight mean for us today?

Over the years, as I have spoken out for justice and peace in small groups, on the streets, on the stage at large demonstrations, within a parish, or on television, I have discovered just how much we do not want to hear the truth. Rarely does the message of disarmament and justice go over well, especially in a time of war. The most dramatic example of that occurred in northern New Mexico, where I was serving as the pastor of five churches, including one small community that consisted almost entirely of retired military families. It was 2003, and the United States had just started its massive bombing campaign on the people of Iraq, a place I had visited a few years earlier. I spoke out against the war all over the country, but also in my parish. Eventually, they organized a meeting of the community, went to the bishop, and asked to have me replaced as their priest. I was quickly removed.

Later, some of them told me that I had divided the parish. From my perspective, it seemed that they had never been more unified! The whole experience was humiliating—and a profound education and blessing. I began to understand the Gospels all over again. From his first public utterance in the Gospel of Luke, back in his home synagogue in Nazareth, Jesus spoke out prophetically and immediately was expelled and almost killed—by

the religious congregation. At every turn, after every announcement of the reign of God, the authorities and the devout wanted
to do away with him. Eventually, they succeeded. At one point,
he lamented bitterly that his very nonviolent presence in such a
world of violence will bring, not peace, but division.

This lesson has long been forgotten by Christian institutions,
from monasteries to parishes to the chanceries. Throughout the
Gospels, Jesus tries to form his followers into prophets who
announce peace to the world of war, and then trains them to
respond nonviolently when the persecution comes down, which
it inevitably will. Today, most Christians, Catholics, priests, and
bishops have learned to avoid the risk of public humiliation and
division for speaking out against war and injustice. They prefer
to keep quiet so that no one gets riled, so that the community
stays as it is, and most importantly, so that the collection baskets
remain full.

But the purpose of the church is not survival but prophecy!

Thomas Merton took this seriously, first of all in his own life
and in his own writing. He spoke out and bore witness with
his solitude and his pen that the Word of God demands peace,
justice, nonviolence, and contemplative prayer. He became a
prophet who announced the Kingdom of God. His life and writings teach that all of us, individually and together as church, are
commanded to announce the kingdom of God, which means
to denounce every war, injustice, weapon, and act of violence
against a human being or creation itself.

Merton became a prophet, and so he has been ignored and
marginalized by most bishops and church leaders. It was a risk
he well understood and gladly accepted. The main thing was to
stay faithful to the Word of God, the gospel of Jesus, and announce it as best he could.

I wish we might all reconsider our faith lives as a sharing
in the prophetic ministry of the church and that we might
together help our local church community to reclaim the prophetic ministry. We need to teach our priests and bishops that
having individual prophets and prophetic parish communities
in every diocese is not only a sign of life and the health of the
church, but a tremendous blessing. In some ways, prophetic
people should be placed at the heart of the church, along with

the poor, the oppressed, and the suffering. Perhaps one day we can help transform the requirements for the office of priest and bishop and the way officials in Rome choose local church leaders, so that the church across every nation and the entire globe can become a prophetic voice for the voiceless, for justice and disarmament, for truth and nonviolence.

Merton's declaration to Jean LeClercq opens up a whole new vista of possibilities for each one of us, for our local church institutions, and for the church as a whole. Let's pray that we might trust in God for our survival, and take up once again the prophetic mission that our Lord has assigned to us.

17

Daniel Berrigan Is Also My Brother

In 1961 poet and Jesuit priest Daniel Berrigan wrote to Merton to thank him for his statement against war in the *Catholic Worker*. Come on down and visit, Merton wrote back. Dan was teaching theology at LeMoyne College in Syracuse, New York, at the time. His first book, *Time without Number*, had recently won the Lamont Poetry Award, and he was widely regarded for his poetry and in demand as a speaker. But he was not yet famous for his stand against war.

As Dan later wrote, he first met Merton in the monastery courtyard. They sat on benches under the large gingko tree. Merton immediately started talking about what it means to be a human being. How can we help people reclaim their humanity? he asked. Dan Berrigan was hooked.

So was Merton. He recognized in Daniel Berrigan a rare peacemaking Christian who was both pastoral and prophetic, wise and witty, compassionate and just. In a letter to a friend afterward, he described Dan as "a man full of fire, the right kind, and a real Jesuit, of which there are not too many perhaps . . . He is alive and full of spirit and truth. I think he will do much for the church in America and so will his brother Phil, the only priest so far to have gone on a Freedom Ride. They will have a hard time, though, and will have to pay for every step forward with their blood."[1]

In *Conjectures of a Guilty Bystander*, Merton reflected further on Dan as "an altogether winning and warm intelligence and a man who, I think, has more than anyone I have ever met the true wide-ranging and simple heart of the Jesuit: zeal, compassion, understanding and uninhibited religious freedom. Just seeing him restores one's hope in the Church."[2]

Merton and Dan corresponded regularly from then on. Each year, Dan visited Gethsemani. When Thich Nhat Hanh visited Merton, one of the first things they did was record a tape for Dan. Sitting in Merton's hermitage, they took turns speaking and then singing for Dan—Merton a Gregorian Alleluia, and Nhat Hanh a Buddhist chant.

Merton had many friends, and over a thousand regular correspondents, from old Columbia classmates like Bob Lax and Ed Rice to poets like Czeslaw Milosz and Denise Levertov, to women religious like Sr. Mary Luke Tobin and Sr. Therese Lentfoehr, to social activists like Dorothy Day and Jim Douglass. I think, however, that Daniel Berrigan, along with Bob Lax, were his closest friends. In Daniel Berrigan, Merton found a peer. They were both priests, poets, writers, peace activists, public figures, and committed church leaders.

Dan would in short time become one of the most famous peacemakers in the world. On May 17, 1968, Dan and Phil Berrigan and seven others poured homemade napalm on hundreds of draft files in Catonsville, Maryland. They were tried and found guilty that October. Dan was at Cornell University, where he was working at the time, when he heard about Merton's sudden death on late-night television news. He grieved so deeply, he later said, that he could not speak about Merton for the next ten years. Dan would eventually spend two years in prison, be featured on the cover of *Time* magazine, write some fifty books, offer lectures and retreats on peace to thousands of people around the world, and engage in serious civil disobedience again in 1980 with his Plowshares disarmament action. Today at age ninety-three and in frail health, he lives in a Jesuit infirmary in New York City.

Their correspondence throughout the 1960s shows how these two Catholic peacemakers encouraged one another in their work for peace. Merton helped Dan remain a Jesuit, especially after his Jesuit superiors sent him to Latin America to stop his public work for peace. Dan helped Merton deepen his nonviolence and resistance, kept him informed about movement events, and counseled him after Roger LaPorte, a young Catholic antiwar activist, immolated himself in New York in protest of the Vietnam War.

They helped each other by first of all encouraging each other. That's what every peacemaker needs—a trusted friend who will encourage you to fulfill your peacemaking vocation. We all need encouragement from like-minded friends if we are going to keep at the struggle for the remainder of our lives.

Tom and Dan also practiced the ancient art of spiritual conversation, which is a key ingredient in the life of gospel nonviolence, especially for anyone who speaks out against war and injustice and who hopes to maintain some semblance of peace, faith, hope, love—even joy. Every peacemaker needs a peacemaking friend with whom they can share their faith, hope, and wisdom, as well as their doubt, despair, and pain, so that both can grow and remain nonviolent. We all need people with whom we can share our belief in God, peace, and nonviolence, and our struggles along the way. By trusting one another and opening up to one another about the deepest spiritual questions, Tom and Dan helped one another to become even better peacemakers and to stay faithful to the way.

Dan Berrigan first wrote to Merton in 1949, after reading *The Seven Storey Mountain*, and then again after Merton's article on peace in the *Catholic Worker*. Merton wrote back on November 10, 1961. That very week Merton seemed to commit himself once and for all to the work of peace and nonviolence, and one of his first actions was to reach out to Dan with friendship and partnership. "Convinced again that I must set everything aside to work for the abolition of war," he wrote in his journal that week. "I remain a contemplative, but as for writing contacts, letters, that kind of effort: here it seems to me everything should yield first place to the struggle against war. This means first of all getting into contact with the others most concerned."[3]

A few days after their initial exchange, Merton committed himself once again to peace: "Yesterday afternoon at the hermitage, surely a decisive clarity came. That I must definitely commit myself to opposition to, and non-cooperation with, nuclear war. That this includes refusing to vote for those who favor the policy of deterrence, and going forward in trying to make this kind of position and its obligation increasingly clear. Not that I did not mean this before, but never so wholly and so definitely."[4]

After Dan's first visit in mid-August 1962, Merton not only praised Dan but recommitted himself to peacemaking:

> Today I realize with urgency the absolute seriousness of my need to study and practice nonviolence. Hitherto I have "liked" nonviolence as an idea. I have "approved" it, looked with benignity upon it, praised it even earnestly. But I have not practiced it fully. My thoughts and words retaliate. I condemn and resist adversaries when I think I am unjustly treated. I revile them. Even treat them with open (but polite) contempt to their face. It is necessary to realize that I am a monk consecrated to God and this restricting non-retaliation merely to physical non-retaliation is not enough; on the contrary it is in some sense a greater evil.
>
> At the same time the energy wasted in contempt, criticism and resentment is thus diverted from its true function, insistence on truth. Hence loss of clarity, loss of focus, confusion and finally frustration . . . I need to set myself to the study of nonviolence with thoroughness. The complete, integral practice of it in community life. Eventually teaching it to others by word and example. Short of this, the monastic life will remain a mockery in my life. It will extend to civil disobedience where necessary. Certainly to non-cooperation in evil, even in monastic policies. But polite, charitable, restrained. I need grace to see how to do this.[5]

As a close friend of Daniel Berrigan for over thirty years, and the author/editor of five books about Dan, I think Merton's encounter with Dan had a powerful disarming effect. Dan has changed the lives of thousands of people, including me, and I submit that Merton was one of them. Disarming and touching the lives of others through a gentle charisma is another part of the peacemaker's life. The above passage is critically important because it reveals a moment when Merton deepened into nonviolence, when he turned a corner in awareness away from the subtleties of inner violence such as holding grudges, feeling negative thoughts toward others, and judging others. Each one of us has to turn that corner at some point in our lives, and then later we understand that we are walking a whole new road of inner peace that must be carefully, consciously followed. Usually, we need other peacemaking friends to help us make that turn.

In his first letter to Dan, Merton cuts right to the chase about the critical importance of working for peace:

> I am very glad to hear that the [peace] movement is getting started in this country and that you are part of it. So am I. We are perhaps very late. Nor should it be regarded as much of a consolation that we are able in some way to salve our consciences by doing something at this hour, even though ineffectual. We must desire to be effective. The greatness of the task is appalling. At moments it seems we are in the middle of a total apostasy, an almost total apostasy from Christ and His teaching. It is not comforting to read the prophets in our night Office these days. . . .
>
> The great problem is the blindness and passivity of Christians and the way they let themselves be used by crypto-fascist elements who get stronger and stronger every day. I have just realized that, as Catholics, we are almost in the same position as the Catholics before the last war in Hitler's Germany. Sometimes too I think we have about five years left to work in, and after that *venit nox*, in whatever form . . . maybe the total *nox*. This one does not go around saying, it seems so foolish. And we are so far from reality. As if the Lord were bound to give us hundreds more years to get some sense in our heads.[6]

From the get-go, Merton shared his deepest Christian concerns with Dan, as if he finally found someone who would not pass out at the harsh truth Merton had discovered. Indeed, with Dan, Merton was finally able to speak about "the unspeakable," his phrase for those unseen systems of evil and death that surround us. He confides in Dan his deepest concern—that we as a people are in the middle of a total apostasy from Christ and his teaching, that we are in the same position as the Catholics in Hitler's Germany. Over fifty years later, I think Merton's hard assessment was proven correct, and we need to face our widespread apostasy to Christ, name it, and work to rediscover a living faith in the God of peace. Every Catholic and Christian needs to heed Merton's warning, return to the nonviolent Jesus and his teachings, renounce every allegiance to the state, and become citizens of God's reign of nonviolence as these two priestly prophets did.

Over the next few years, Merton continued to share his own struggles with Dan. Here are two examples:

I realize that I am about at the end of some kind of line. What line? What is the trolley I am probably getting off? The trolley is called a special kind of hope. The streetcar of expectation, of things becoming much more intelligible, of things being set in a new kind of order, and so on. Point one, things are not going to get better. Point two, things are going to get worse. I will not dwell on point two. Point three, I don't need to be on the trolley car anyway. I don't belong riding in a trolley. You can call the trolley anything you like, I have got off it. You can call the trolley a form of religious leprosy if you like. It is burning out. In a lot of sweat and pain if you like but it is burning out for real. The leprosy of that particular kind of temporal hope . . . I am sick up to the teeth and beyond the teeth, up to the eyes and beyond the eyes, with all forms of projects and expectations and statements and programs and explana-tions of anything, especially explanations about where we are all going, because where we are all going is where we went a long time ago, over the falls. We are in a new river and we don't know it.[7]

&

There are chances I might be able to move to a real wild place five or six miles away. A completely hidden valley where nobody but hunters ever go, and the thing about it, two things—quite symbolic—first slaves used to live there and second, the SAC plane goes over sometimes five or six times a day real low so you can look right up at the bomb bay and get your mind on what you are there for. Composition of place made easy . . . The Vietnam thing is sickening and just about as stupid as one would imagine possible, but I have an odd feeling that it is not going to get any more intelligent as time goes on. This country seems to be bent on giving everyone for all time a clear lesson in how to miss all one's opportunities to make a good use of power.[8]

In Dan, Merton found another trusted friend. In Merton, Dan found a spiritual adviser. He wrote repeatedly for advice, especially as he began to speak out and take public action against the U.S. war in Vietnam. For example, one of Dan's 1965 letters to Merton begins as follows: "Just a short note with a loud cry like the Beatles: 'Help!' " Merton readily responded in many letters to Dan, offering his wisdom, advice that we as peacemakers can all take to heart:

If one reads the prophets with his ears and eyes open he cannot help recognizing his obligation to shout very loud about God's will, God's truth and justice of humanity to humanity... What is the contemplative life if one doesn't listen to God in it? What is the contemplative life if one becomes oblivious to the rights of men and women and the truth of God in the world and in his Church?[9]

Do not be discouraged. The Holy Spirit is not asleep. Nor let yourself get too frustrated. There is no use getting mad at the Church and her representatives. First there is the problem of communication, which is impossible. Then there is the fact that God writes straight on crooked lines anyway, all the time, all the time. The lines are crooked enough by now. And we I suppose are what he is writing with, though we can't see what is being written. And what he writes is not for peace of soul, that is sure.[10]

᷼

You are going to be able to do a great deal of good simply stating facts quietly and telling the truth quietly and patiently. With so much obvious truth on your side and with enough honesty around to keep people open and interested, you should not have too much trouble.[11]

᷼

The real job is to lay the groundwork for a deep change of heart on the part of the whole nation so that one day it can really go through the metanoia we need for a peaceful world.[12]

᷼

In my opinion the job of the Christian is to try to give an example of sanity, independence, human integrity, good sense, as well as Christian love and wisdom, against all establishments and all mass movements and all current fashions which are merely mindless and hysterical.[13]

Note the basics of gospel peacemaking from one of the most famous monks in history to someone who would become one of the most famous peacemaking priests in history: *Shout very loud about God's will, God's truth, God's justice. State facts quietly and tell the truth quietly and patiently. Don't be discouraged. Don't get too frustrated. Don't get mad at the Church and her representatives. Lay the groundwork for a deep change of heart. Give an example of sanity, independence, integrity, good sense, as well as Christian love and wisdom.*

Dan went on to live these teachings for the rest of his life and became a model peacemaker. We, too, can take Merton's spiritual advice to heart and spend the rest of our lives becoming model peacemakers.

18

Robert Lax, Friend and Peacemaker

A brief interlude is called for. We cannot reflect on the peace-making life of Thomas Merton without mention of one other key person—Robert Lax, Merton's oldest and best friend.

Born a Jew, Lax befriended Merton at Columbia University and converted to Catholicism, too, five years after Merton. After teaching for a while, Lax worked as an editor at *Time* magazine and the *New Yorker*, as a Hollywood screenwriter, as a reporter for the progressive Catholic magazine *Jubilee*, and even as a circus clown. Lax's dear friend Jack Kerouac called him "a laughing Buddha." Living in Greenwich Village in the late 1950s and early 1960s, Lax befriended Bob Dylan and was with him the night he wrote "Blowin' in the Wind." Later he knew Padre Pio. Like Merton, Lax was in constant touch with a wide array of artists, writers, and thinkers.

Lax is still barely known in America, except in Merton studies, but his poetry has been widely read throughout Europe for decades. His book of poems, *Circus of the Sun*, which compares creation to a circus, was called "perhaps the greatest English language poem of this century" by the *New York Times Book Review*. Another reviewer considered him the best poet after T. S. Eliot.

"Lax was born with the deepest sense of who God was," Thomas Merton once wrote. "He was much wiser than I, and he had clearer vision, and was, in fact, corresponding much more truly to the grace of God than I. He had seen what was the one important thing."

In a memorable scene in *The Seven Storey Mountain*, Lax

and Merton are walking down Fifth Avenue one day when Lax asks, "What do you want to be anyway?"

Merton hesitates and says, "I guess I want to be a good Catholic."

"What you should say," Lax declares, "is that you want to be a saint."

"How do you expect me to be a saint?" Merton asks.

"By wanting to," Lax answers. "All that is necessary to be a saint is to want to be one. All you have to do is desire it."[1]

That conversation set Merton's heart and mind on a long search that took him to Gethsemani. Lax, on the other hand, seems to have achieved a palpable holiness at an early age. Merton admired Lax immensely and hoped to visit with him in Greece on his return from Asia. Their hilarious friendship comes through in the recently published collection of their zany letters, called *If Prophecy Still Had a Voice*. Both Lax and Merton willed themselves to become saints and peacemakers.

One day in the mid-1990s I received a letter from Patmos, Greece. It began,

Dear John, I've been following you for years. No one in the world seems to work harder for peace, and I feel sorry for you because things seem to be getting so much worse. Quick, drop everything. Take the enclosed ten dollar bill, go immediately to the nearest pub and buy yourself a big, tall beer and drink it on me. My treat. We are together in the journey and life of peace.

The letter was signed by Robert Lax.

I remember staring in disbelief at the ten-dollar bill that had traveled so far. I was thrilled to hear from the great poet, who I knew had famously left the United States in 1962 to live in exile, solitude, and peace as a hermit first on Kalymnos, then on Patmos, near the cave where Saint John the Evangelist may have written the book of Revelation.

I wrote back, and we became friends through correspondence. I sent him regular care packages of books, articles, and peace materials until his death on September 26, 2000.

Recently, a beautiful book was published about Robert Lax. *The Way of the Dreamcatcher: Spirit Lessons with Robert Lax, Poet, Peacemaker and Sage* by Steve Georgiou celebrates Lax's peacemaking life through interviews, reflections, and poetry. The original Novalis edition (now out of print) includes stunning color photographs of the young author with the wise old poet standing before the cobalt-blue Aegean Sea. The photos bring Lax and his wisdom to life.

Thanks to Georgiou, whom I know from the International Thomas Merton Society, we finally learn why Merton and so many others considered Lax a true contemplative, mystic, and saint. Here for the first time we get a glimpse into his peaceful mind, heart, and spirit. In effect, we learn why Merton looked up to Lax, how Lax modeled the life of faith and wisdom for Merton, and what Merton learned about peacemaking from Lax.

Steve tells an amazing anecdote of wandering around Patmos in 1993, unaware of Lax or even Merton, when a young man he met urged him to go meet the village poet because he thought they would have much in common. Steve knocked on Lax's door. Lax let him in, and so began a long, fruitful friendship that led to a series of interviews and eventually this beautiful tribute.

"We are meant to be holy, all of us," Lax told Steve Georgiou. "We're all called to be saints."

Lax's advice to the young graduate student is short and simple: "Relax," "Slow down," "Simplify," "Love everyone unconditionally."

"Every day I try to find out more about the spirit of peace within myself," Lax told Steve. "Everything I do now, I try to relate it with that. Writing is my craft, and if I can in any way cultivate peace through it, then I'm happy.... Who knows what one loving act can do? Who can trace the measure of a single peaceful word said from the heart?"[2]

Throughout these conversations, Lax sounds like a Catholic Zen master, and like Steve Georgiou, I'm glad to hear the lessons of peace from Lax, who first taught them to Merton. Here are excerpts from Lax's peacemaking lessons.

Unconditional love. That's the bottom line. Everything is here because of love. That's why we were created—to love. Love keeps things going, not just for now, but forever. Love gives life and makes sure what's around today will be around tomorrow. It's all about compassion. That's what the cosmos best responds to.

❧

Every moment is a gift. Relax, get into the moment, and do all you can to listen to it. I mean, really, really listen. Be present to the moment with everything you are.

❧

It takes practice. After you've listened for a while, you start responding. I think you start working your gifts in response to what you've heard. You become appreciative of the moment. You give back because you begin to see how everything is on loan, a gift from God.

❧

Learn how to look. Take time to look to see what's right there in front of you, to let what you see sink in. When you look at a flower opening or a tree moving with the wind, you just relax and take it all in. Try and see everything like that, if you can.

❧

Looking and listening lead into everything. . . . You become more totally aware of reality. It's so true—everything we need to live well is already within our possession. Wisdom is right before our very eyes.

❧

Jesus doesn't tell me to hate or to kill. He tells me to love. More and more, I'm emphasizing the power of peace. So many good and lasting things proceed from peace.

❧

You shouldn't fight fire with fire; you address fire with water. And the water is agape, nonviolence. Cruel people are still people, but they have somehow forgotten how to love. Being cruel to them will only reinforce their cruelty.

❧

But what might kindness do? What might peacefulness do? I think that's what Jesus was thinking about.

❧

Be gentle and patient both with yourself and with others, no matter what comes along. In this way, waiting becomes a fulfilling, very meaningful experience. If you live gently, honorably, focusing on the cultivation of your heart, good things are sure to follow.

❧

Prayer is a way of doing instantaneous good for all things in all places. It's a way of sending out love everywhere at once. It's a power that everyone has access to, and it can transfigure the world. Prayer makes everything you do more real, lasting, meaningful and fruitful. Through prayer, everything just flowers and flows.

❧

Try to live as purely and as simply and as gently as you can. Relax. Be flexible. Be forgiving. Be creative. Be loving. You are a peacemaker. Those who cross your path may need you.

❧

Listen, be discerning, use all the radar you can generate in your waking moments. Try to keep the balance. The whole world's watching, counting on you to do the right thing, the loving thing. So let in the light whenever, wherever you can.[3]

Lax was the real thing, a rare contemplative and solitary who spent his life, like Merton, in poverty, silence, reading, writing, and meditating. He was a great peacemaker.

"The greatest thing you can do in this life is to cultivate and exercise compassion," Bob Lax told Steve Georgiou. "Life is about learning how to flow with your basic goodness. It's about entering the heart and making it the fount of your being."

Bob Lax knew Thomas Merton the longest and the best. He took Merton's lessons of peace to heart, but maybe it was the other way around. In either case, he shows us how to follow the example of Thomas Merton and become a fount of peace, love, nonviolence, and compassion.

Here's to you, Bob, and thanks!

19

A Chant for Peace

Merton's creative nonviolence, spiritual searching, and adamant truth-telling led him to explore different angles of writing to name the unspeakable horrors of our time in order to awaken the conscience of the faithful. In the early 1960s he addressed the diabolic violence of the Nazis in a devastating poem using the voice of a Nazi commander who celebrates his obedient work for the state. The commander speaks proudly of leading millions to the gas chambers and cremation ovens as if it were a devotional act, an act of piety, service, even nobility. But then, in the last line, Merton pulls the rug out from under the reader, holding up a mirror to our own crimes and hypocrisy.

"Chant to Be Used in Processions around a Site with Furnaces" first appeared in the *Catholic Worker*. From its opening line, it shocked readers. This was not the pious Thomas Merton loved by millions. It was a brave, new, bold Merton, one who pushed the truth in our faces. And yet he did it without self-righteousness or judgment. He just laid out the truth, when we least expected it. After a lifetime of contemplative prayer, he could do no less. He had to address systemic evil and name it as such, whether by German Nazis or American warmakers. It begins,

How we made them sleep and purified them
How we perfectly cleaned up the people and worked a
  big heater
I was the commander I made improvements and
  installed a guaranteed system taking account of

human weakness I purified and I remained decent
How I commanded
I made cleaning appointments and then I made the
    travelers sleep and after that I made soap
I was born into a Catholic family but as these people
    were not going to need a priest I did not become a
    priest I installed a perfectly good machine it gave
    satisfaction to many
When trains arrived the soiled passengers received
    appointments for fun in the bathroom they did not
    guess
It was a very big bathroom for two thousand people it
    awaited arrival and they arrived safely[1]

On he goes, taking us through the civic duty of the commander,
into the horror of genocide, as if it were normal, reasonable,
even praiseworthy.

Point: The murder of millions of people was orchestrated by
ordinary, obedient, patriotic citizens, most of them Catholic and
Christian, who set aside any measure of decency or basic humanity to do whatever the state said, including throwing people into
the death house. Obedience to the state was the highest good,
one's holy duty. It was never questioned. Millions died while
millions more obediently served their state. He continues,

All the while I had obeyed perfectly
So I was hanged in a commanding position with a full
    view of the site plant and grounds
You smile at my career but you would do as I did if
    you knew yourself and dared
In my day we worked hard we saw what we did our
    self sacrifice was conscientious and complete our
    work was faultless and detailed[2]

Then the punch line:

Do not think yourself better because you burn up
    friends and enemies with long-range missiles without
    ever seeing what you have done[3]

Do not think yourself better! But that's exactly what we think! We are not mad Nazis, we have not committed genocide, we're not anti-Semitic, mass murderers.

Maybe not, but we still serve the forces of death. We, too, bring good people to death, by the millions. Whether we force people in cremation ovens or napalm people in Vietnam or arm death squads in Central America or fund the Israeli occupation of Palestinians or ignore apartheid for decades or support corporate greed while millions starve to death or drop untold tons of bombs on Iraqis or use unmanned drones to kill civilians in Afghanistan, Pakistan, and Yemen—we, too, obediently serve death. We go along with our civic duty. We support the troops, wave the flag, do our patriotic duty, and through our government, kill millions.

You have so arranged your killing, the Nazi commander says to us, that you do not know what you have done. With nuclear weapons, you vaporized hundreds of thousands in Hiroshima and Nagasaki. With bombs dropped from the highest altitudes, you blew up entire villages, families, and communities in Vietnam and Iraq. Now with your unmanned drones that fly thousands of miles around the globe, you kill ordinary people and don't even know you wage war. The United States has killed millions of people over the last century, and continues to kill, but we rarely see the effects of our killing. So we look the other way and forget what our military is doing.

Though the methods may differ, it still means death to ordinary civilians. Whether through gas chambers, nuclear weapons, long-range missiles, or unmanned drones, it still means death. You might have figured out a way not to see the effects of mass murder—your number-one business, the Nazi commander tells us—but you, too, are guilty of crimes against humanity. The time has come to recognize your complicity with death and repent.

Merton would never put it so baldly, yet that horrific anti-poem should sting every reader and push our conscience into action.

Merton's lifelong "chant for peace" had to include such shocking "chants for war." Through poetry, he helps us swallow this bitter pill and coaxes us to open our eyes to our own systemic violence. In doing so, he addresses the question forced upon every American who dares become a peacemaker: "But what about Hitler?" Over the course of a lifetime, Merton had invited us into the presence of the God of peace, to live out Jesus's teachings of peace, and to become people of contemplative prayer as a spiritual antidote to the world's wars. But now he names evil for what it is, lifting up the responsibility of nonviolent resistance to evil. He did his research and pointed out how nonviolent resistance to state-sanctioned evil, even against the Nazis, always works.

In his essay "Danish Resistance to Hitler," Merton explained how active nonviolent resistance in Denmark prevented the Nazi extermination of Jews. "Denmark was one of the only nations which offered explicit, formal and successful nonviolent resistance to Nazi power," Merton writes, although he could have also written about Norwegian and Bulgarian resistance. "The resistance was successful because it was explicit and formal, and because it was, practically speaking, unanimous. The entire Danish nation simply refused to cooperate with the Nazis, and resisted every move of the Nazis against the Jews with nonviolent protest of the highest and most effective caliber."[4] He continues,

> The Danish nation, from the king on down, formally and publicly rejected the [Nazi] policy and opposed it with an open, calm, convinced resistance which shook the morale of the German troops and SS men occupying the country and changed their whole outlook on the Jewish question. When the Germans first approached the Danes about the segregation of Jews, proposing the introduction of the yellow badge, government officials replied that the King of Denmark would be the first to wear the badge. . . . It was the only nation which as a whole expressed a forthright moral objection to [Nazi] policy.[5]

Merton details how the Danes used strikes, demonstrations, underground smuggling operations, and public denunciations to protect Jews and resist Nazis. He even concludes that forty-eight Jews died in Nazi hands, most of them from natural causes, as compared to the hundreds of thousands of Jews who died in each of the surrounding nations. Merton goes on to ask how can so many Christians who think they live by "a humanistic standard" or "the Christian ethic" "rationalize a conscious, uninterrupted and complete cooperation in activities which we now see to have been not only criminal but diabolical."

"Why did a course of action which worked so simply and so well in Denmark not occur to all the other so-called Christian nations of the West just as simply and just as spontaneously?" Merton asks. This serious question is one worth the study of every peacemaker. As Merton suggests through poetry, we are not living under Nazi rule, but under the U.S. government, now in the twenty-first century, which kills civilians around the world and threatens the whole planet with its nuclear arsenal and environmental destruction. "Such action [as the Danes] becomes possible where fundamental truths are taken seriously," Merton concludes.[6]

By examining such questions, Merton showed the power of active nonviolence in movements and entire nations. Fifty years later, after some eighty-five documented nonviolent revolutions and hundreds of successful nonviolent movements against injustice, there are hundreds of new history books that document and explain how nonviolent resistance to state-sanctioned murder can work in movements and nations. Like Merton, we, too, need to study the history of nonviolence, in its resistance to the Nazis as well as in movements from the suffragists to civil rights, up to today such as in Liberia's revolutionary nonviolence, the Singing Revolution of Estonia, and the Arab Spring. Along the way we realize that when it is tried, it works. Organized nonviolent resistance is not just an ideal but a realistic, effective alternative, as the historical research now proves.

Besides arguing that organized nonviolent resistance could work even against the Nazis, Merton turned to an unknown Catholic from Austria to point out the ultimate Christian response to systemic evil, even by Nazis. Instead of highlighting the beloved theologian Dietrich Bonhoeffer, who in the end assisted in the plot to assassinate Hitler, Merton focused on Franz Jägerstätter, a devout farmer who was literally one of the only Austrians to refuse to fight for Hitler. Few people had ever heard of Jägerstätter when Merton wrote about him, but in Austria, Jägerstätter was still regarded as a traitor. Merton's reflections legitimated Jägerstätter's stand and made him a noble example to conscientious objectors and the nascent U.S. peace movement.

Jägerstätter refused to sign the oath to support Nazi rule, citing his Catholic faith and allegiance to Jesus. Everyone tried to talk him out of his "fanatic" Christianity, including his parish priest and local bishop. But he refused, was arrested, carted off to Berlin, tried, and beheaded within six months. He left behind his devoted young wife, Franziska, and three little girls.

"The story of the Austrian peasant is plainly that of a martyr, and of a Christian who followed a path of virtue with a dedication that cannot be fully accounted for by human motivation alone," Merton writes in his essay "An Enemy of the State." "The real question raised by the Jägerstätter story," he concludes, "is not merely that of the individual Catholic's right to conscientious objection, but the question of the Church's own mission of protest and prophecy in the gravest spiritual crisis humanity has ever known."[7]

Merton was the first major church figure to write about nonviolent resistance to the Nazis and Franz Jägerstätter (drawing on the classic book by Gordon Zahn, *In Solitary Witness*). Merton's essay had a huge impact on many, including me. It helped my determination to resist war with the same dedication of Jägerstätter and Merton. I knew I wouldn't be killed, but I might be imprisoned, as indeed I later was. In the late 1990s, after I was released from jail for a Plowshares disarmament action, I journeyed to Jägerstätter's home village of St. Radegund, on the Austrian-German border. There I spent a week with Franziska Jägerstätter and her family. It was just over fifty years since his execution. She told me her story and brought down his prison letters, which she kept in a shoebox under her bed, to show me. I specifically told her about Merton's essay, which I first read in 1980, and how Merton's writing on Franz inspired me and many other peace activists across the United States to take a public stand against war—and to do so as a Catholic.

In 2007 I flew back to Austria to take part in the celebratory Mass for Franz's beatification in Linz, which was broadcast live on national TV. Franziska was overjoyed and found it hard to take in, given decades of rejection from everyone in Austria, including church leaders. Merton would scarcely believe it, too, if he was alive, and yet this is precisely the person the church should be honoring. Merton played a huge part in supporting Jägerstätter's witness and its eventual acceptance by the institutional church.

In the age of permanent warfare, genocide, and nuclear weapons, Franz Jägerstätter has become the epitome of the Christian witness. He adhered to the nonviolence of Jesus, come what may. Even when everything was hopeless, he proclaimed that it is better to die without arms, like Christ, than with them. In this, he surpasses even Bonhoeffer, the great theologian, who went to his death confessing that he had participated in mortal sin, not costly grace. An hour before he was killed, Jägerstätter told a visiting priest that he did not need help because he was in "perfect union with Jesus and Mary." Franz was a prophet and martyr, but also a saint and mystic. He shows us what we could be.

Thomas Merton does the same. Like Merton, our vocation will probably not include martyrdom, but it certainly does include prophecy and mysticism. We, too, can denounce warmaking, support nonviolent resistance, and uphold martyrs like Jägerstätter and encourage others to aspire to the nonviolence of Jesus.

In the age of permanent warfare, terrorism, extreme poverty, and catastrophic climate change, Merton's assessment of the church's call to "protest and prophecy" still goes unheard. He summons each one of us to do what we can, whether like the Danes or Jägerstätter or Merton himself, to engage in public protest and prophetic speaking and writing on behalf of the nonviolence of Jesus and God's reign of peace.

20

The Sane Ones

The great Italian novelist Ignacio Silone, author of *Bread and Wine*, once wrote, "It is difficult, but it is necessary, above all, to know who is insane and who is not."

Merton would agree. In a world where peace advocates are dismissed as fanatics while nuclear weapons manufacturers, military generals, and murdering soldiers are treated as heroes, one begins to wonder who is sane and who is not.

"The real problem," Merton wrote in *Faith and Violence*, "is not the individual with a revolver, but death and even genocide as big business. This big business of death is all the more innocent and effective because it involves a long chain of individuals, each of whom can feel himself absolved from responsibility, and each of whom can perhaps salve his conscience by contributing with a more meticulous efficiency to his part in the massive operation."[1]

As Merton matured in his understanding of the contemplative life and its prophetic dimension, he began to name systemic, structured, institutionalized violence as the ultimate evil, and he called the church to renounce its complicity with these forces. He looked hard at "the big business of death" to better understand our predicament and point a way out.

As a case study, after reading Hannah Arendt's *The Banality of Evil*, Merton wrote passionately about Adolf Eichmann, the Nazi official who oversaw the extermination of millions of Jews and felt no guilt whatsoever. Merton noted that Eichmann and others felt justified in organizing genocide "due partly to their absolute obedience to the higher authority and partly to the care and efficiency which went into the details of their work. This was done almost entirely on paper. Since they dealt with numbers, not with people, and since their job was one of abstract bureaucratic organization, apparently, they could easily forget the reality of what they were doing." Merton continued,

> The same is true to an even greater extent in modern warfare in which the real moral problems are not to be located in rare instances of hand-to-hand combat, but in the remote planning and organization of technological destruction. The real crimes of modern war are committed not at the front but in war offices and ministries of defense in which no one ever has to see any blood unless his secretary gets a nosebleed. Modern technological mass murder is not directly visible, like individual murder. It is abstract, corporate, businesslike, cool, free of guilt feelings and therefore a thousand times more deadly and effective than the eruption of violence out of individual hate. It is this polite, massively organized, white-collar murder machine that threatens the world with destruction, not the violence of a few desperate teenagers in a slum.[2]

In "A Devout Meditation on Eichmann," Merton pondered Eichmann's cold, calculated, businesslike approach to genocide and realized that the big business of death had become normalized. Merton was shocked that just before Eichmann's trial, a psychiatrist pronounced him "perfectly sane." "Now it begins to dawn on us that it is precisely the sane ones who are the most dangerous." He continues,

> It is the sane ones, the well-adapted ones, who can without qualms and without nausea aim the missiles and press the buttons that will initiate the great festival of destruction that they, the sane ones, have prepared. . . . No one suspects the sane, and the sane ones will have perfectly good reasons, logical, well-adjusted reasons, for firing the shot. They will be obeying sane orders that have come sanely down the chain of command. And because of their sanity

they will have no qualms at all. When the missiles take off, then, it will be no mistake.[3]

"The whole concept of sanity in a society where spiritual values have lost their meaning is itself meaningless." Merton continued,

> Eichmann was sane. The generals and fighters on both sides, in World War II, the ones who carried out the total destruction of entire cities, these were the sane ones. Those who invented and developed atomic bombs, nuclear weapons, missiles; who have planned the strategy of the next war; who have evaluated the various possibilities of using bacterial and chemical agents: these are not the crazy people, they are the sane people. The ones who coolly estimate how many millions of victims can be considered expendable in a nuclear war, I presume they do all right with the Rorschach ink blots too. On the other hand, you will probably find that the pacifists and the ban-the-bomb people are, quite seriously, just as we read in *Time*, a little crazy.[4]

Merton struggles to articulate the insanity of working for genocide, weapons of mass destruction, or war. Life is so precious, so fragile, so beautiful, so holy, he might add, "Why would anyone waste it serving the forces of death? How could anyone participate in the big business of death? They must be pathologically insane. They have no sense of empathy or compassion." We have lost any feeling for those who suffer or will suffer from our warmaking. Given the widespread support of war, nuclear weapons, and bombing raids, one could argue that society is full of sociopaths.

One can only imagine what Merton would say about the current U.S. drone strikes over Pakistan and Yemen, the U.S. funding of the Israeli occupation of Palestine and massacre of children in Gaza, the unprecedented U.S. bombing raids of Iraq and fourteen-year-war and military occupation of Afghanistan, and the myth of a permanent war on terrorism.

What are the human, spiritual consequences of our businesslike preparations for nuclear war, our drone flights and unmanned bombing raids that kill civilians and children thousands of miles away, our Trident submarines that can vaporize millions in minutes quietly prowling the oceans, and the giant corporations that keep billions impoverished and destroy the earth? When insanity becomes sanity, and the sanity of peace is dismissed as unrealistic, we have not only lost our conscious minds but our souls. We have renounced the living God and mindful peace and moved into society-wide mindlessness and violence.

Gandhi once wrote that nonviolence is the highest form of conscious living. Merton concluded that sanity comes from nonviolence and mindfulness. We can measure our sanity, he might say, by the level of our nonviolence. Further, sanity is a prerequisite for authentic faith.

If we want to serve the God of life, we cannot serve the big business of death. If we want to serve the God of peace, we cannot serve the culture of war. If we want to be people of the God of life, peace, and love, we see every human being as a sister and brother, and reach out with universal, nonviolent love that all might have the fullness of life and peace.

21

Original Child Bomb

In another creative leap, Merton set out, through a "found" poem, to tell the story of the making of the atomic bomb and how the United States used it on Hiroshima and Nagasaki. Published as a small book, *Original Child Bomb* walks us through the story and, in doing so, educates us to the insanity of nuclear weapons. Merton argues, like Gandhi, that addressing and working to abolish nuclear weapons is a requirement of the contemplative life. Spiritual seekers should lead the way in the campaigns to rid the world of these horrific weapons, which can undo in fifteen minutes what the Creator spent billions of years to create. If this is not the subject of our contemplation and attention, Merton would say we have missed the whole point.

"In the year 1945, an Original Child was born," Merton writes. "The name Original Child was given to it by the Japanese people, who recognized that it was the first of its kind."[1] Using stark sentences and short numbered paragraphs, Merton's anti-poem focuses on Truman's decision to use the bomb. "About one hour after Mr. Truman became President, his aides told him about a new bomb," he continues. "One of those present added, in a reverent tone, that the new explosive might eventually destroy the whole world." Some told the president that "the new bomb would end the war and bring eternal peace." It goes on:

The time was coming for the new bomb to be tested, in the New Mexico desert. A name was chosen to designate this secret operation. It was called "Trinity."

At 5:30 a.m. on July 16th, 1945, a plutonium bomb was successfully exploded in the desert at Alamogordo, New Mexico. . . .

Many who saw the experiment expressed their satisfaction in religious terms. A semi-official report even quoted a religious book—The New Testament—"Lord, I believe, help thou my unbelief." There was an atmosphere of devotion. It was a great act of faith.[2]

&

On Sunday afternoon "Little Boy" was brought out in procession and devoutly tucked away in the womb of Enola Gay. That evening few were able to sleep. They were as excited as little boys on Christmas eve.[3]

&

The bomb exploded within 100 feet of the aiming point. The fireball was 18,000 feet across. The temperature at the center of the fireball was 100,000,000 degrees. The people who were near the center became nothing. The whole city was blown to bits and the ruins all caught fire instantly everywhere, burning briskly. 70,000 people were killed right away or died within a few hours. Those who did not die at once suffered great pain. Few of them were soldiers.[4]

On August 9th another bomb was dropped on Nagasaki, though Hiroshima was still burning.

As to the Original Child that was now born, President Truman summed up the philosophy of the situation in a few words. "We found the bomb," he said, "and we used it."[5]

Merton tells the story with simple factual statements without judgment, as if the building and use of the bomb were perfectly normal, reasonable, and right. He ends as follows:

Since that summer many other bombs have been "found." What is going to happen? At the time of writing, after a season of brisk speculation, men seem to be fatigued by the whole question.[6]

Seventy years after Hiroshima and Nagasaki, many other bombs have been "found." We have made tens of thousands of them, most of them far more destructive than the Hiroshima bomb. We exploded thousands of them in above-ground and underground "tests," almost dropped them on ourselves several times, and have come close to using our nuclear weapons dozens of times, most infamously during the Cuban missile crisis of October 1962. We now know, too, what Merton did not know—that we dropped those atomic bombs not to end the war (the United States knew that the Japanese were about to surrender), but to impress the Soviet Union with our military power so that we would emerge from World War II as the world's new superpower. Instead, the U.S. atomic bombing of Hiroshima led to the Cold War. One could argue that the war never ended. The world has remained on hair-trigger alert. We still have the capacity to destroy the whole planet. Things are worse than ever, and people are still "fatigued."

Fifty years ago, the United States, the Soviet Union, Britain, France, and China signed the international Nuclear Non-Proliferation Treaty (NPT). They agreed to work to end the arms race and abolish nuclear weapons. Today at least four more states have nuclear weapons—Israel, India, Pakistan, and North Korea—and many others are trying to develop them. But all these nations have failed to reduce nuclear weapons. The treaty has been ignored, and no nation pursues the abolition of nuclear weapons. Trillions of dollars have been wasted in preparation for nuclear war, while billions starve and suffer in poverty, the environment continues to be poisoned, and other wars and terrorist acts continue. We are as unsafe as ever, maybe even closer to nuclear war than ever.

Nuclear weapons remain the most dangerous things on earth. They're bad for children, bad for the environment, bad for our health, bad for the economy, bad for the poor, bad for our security, and bad for our souls—and yet people are "fatigued" about the whole question.

We may never be able to clean up the environment or feed the world's hungry until we abolish these weapons once and for all. Then we can use those billions of dollars wisely to meet real human needs and establish real security and peace. Merton did his part to wake us up to the urgent need for nuclear disarmament. He tried to break through our apathy by writing long essays against nuclear weapons, countless letters to friends far and wide, and this famous "found" poem. After the Vietnam War, the antinuclear movement grew in the late 1970s, a million people marched in New York City's Central Park in 1982, and a hundred Plowshares disarmament actions occurred at nuclear and military installations around the United States and the world. But today, however, few speak out against nuclear weapons. Hardly any politician calls for their abolition. Most have given up any hope. We have made peace with nuclear war. With hell on earth.

In the high desert of New Mexico where I live, where Merton visited twice before his death, I see the hidden mountaintop of Los Alamos, where the U.S. National Nuclear Weapons Laboratories churn out ever more nuclear weapons. Every year, hundreds of us trek up the mountain to remember the U.S. atomic bombings of Hiroshima and Nagasaki. Sometimes the media covers our event, sometimes not, but we keep going. Business is booming at Los Alamos. At this writing, President Barack Obama and the U.S. government still hope to rebuild Los Alamos and create a new, state-of-the-art plutonium bomb factory, for the hefty price of $4 billion. New Mexico is the poorest state in the nation and recently achieved the distinction of returning to first place in child hunger, but we keep on building nuclear weapons.

We go there once a year to pray and speak out against nuclear weapons, and for the coming of a nuclear-free world of peace with justice. It's not much, but it does break through the fatigue, the silence, the apathy that paralyze us. If more of us stand up and speak out, it could mean the difference between life and death. That's what Merton was telling us.

Nuclear weapons are our modern idols. They are not golden calves that we worship; they are far worse. They cost billions, trillions over decades. And we place all our security, hope, safety, and trust in them—not in the God of peace. Their very existence shows our lack of faith, hope, and love.

After the atomic bombing of Hiroshima, Gandhi said simply, "We have seen what nuclear weapons have done to the Japanese. It is too early to see what this has done to the soul of those who used them."

At Los Alamos, we see the effect. We rush ahead building ever more nuclear weapons, yet we have lost our souls. Los Alamos is a city right out of the movies, such as *Night of the Living Dead* or *Invasion of the Body Snatchers*. It is a lifeless place, where people run around, make money, and serve the false gods of death.

If we want to reclaim our souls and maintain some kind of spiritual life, we have to break our complicity with these weapons of mass destruction. If we want others to end their apathy, we have to end ours. How to break through apathy and become nonapathetic people who care about others, who care about peace, love, compassion, nonviolence, and the whole human family? That means speaking out against weapons of mass destruction, praying and fasting for their abolition, attending and organizing nonviolent demonstrations, demanding our political leaders abolish these weapons, and doing what we can to support the grassroots movement of nuclear disarmament. Just as our ancestors worked to abolish slavery, we have to work to abolish nuclear weapons. Even if we do not live to see their abolition, we have to give our lives for that cause.

Fatigue? Merton says we need to wake up now to reality. No more sleeping. No more fatigue. No more apathy. We believe in the God of peace. We place our hope, our faith, our security, our trust in the God of peace. We are alive, here and now, in the present moment of peace. And so we do what we can, like Merton, to wake others up, to end the fatigue, to hasten a new nuclear-free world.

22

Living With Wisdom, Our Feminine God

In 1962 Merton published his masterpiece prose poem, *Hagia Sophia*, to celebrate holy Wisdom as the feminine manifestation of God. He described Sophia as the feminine child playing before God at all times and in the world, but also as "unfathomable mercy, made manifest in the world by means of the incarnation, death and resurrection of Jesus Christ."[1]

Theologian Christopher Pramuk calls *Hagia Sophia* "a classic of modern Christian mysticism." "Against a century of unspeakable violence and dehumanization, *Hagia Sophia* is Merton's consummate hymn to the theological dignity of humankind and of all creation," Pramuk writes.[2] "It is a hymn of awakening, a hymn to peace, a call to peace."[3] It begins,

> There is in all visible things an invisible fecundity, a dimmed light, a meek namelessness, a hidden wholeness. This mysterious Unity and Integrity is Wisdom, the Mother of all, Natura naturans. There is in all things an inexhaustible sweetness and purity, a silence that is a fount of action and joy. It rises up in wordless gentleness and flows out to me from the unseen roots of all created being.[4]

A few years ago Pramuk published *Sophia: The Hidden Christ of Thomas Merton*, in which he suggested that Merton's turn toward *Hagia Sophia*, Holy Wisdom—the feminine side of God,

130

or Christ as the Wisdom of God—took him unexpectedly deeper into the mystery of the divine, enabling him to name the realities of "The Unspeakable," all the while becoming more nonviolent, more compassionate, and more human. The most original and creative commentator on Merton in decades, Pramuk suggests that this discovery of Holy Wisdom transformed Merton into a peacemaker, and that if we seek the Wisdom of God, our own spiritual journey to peace will deepen and bear good fruit for the world.

Because Merton sought the God of peace so diligently, it is not surprising in hindsight that this monk and poet would take the biblical theme of Wisdom so seriously. Few Western Christian writers of the time wrote about Holy Wisdom—perhaps because it was the domain of the Eastern churches, perhaps because Christian men never addressed the feminine side of God. But as Merton turned toward the world in 1960, he did so in the company of Holy Wisdom. Eventually he described his life in the woods as "living with Wisdom." This became for him the highest manifestation of the life of peace.

Through his constant Bible study, regular liturgical prayer, daily silent meditation, and even his dreams, Merton encountered God as Wisdom. On the one hand, this discovery opened up the feminine side of God, but he knew that Holy Wisdom was one of the titles for Christ in Orthodox Christianity. The feminine Wisdom disarmed Merton and gave him new eyes to see with mercy and compassion the world of violence and war. Because of Holy Wisdom he practiced and taught Christian nonviolence and advocated the wisdom of peace to the world. He experienced God as Wisdom, so he was inspired to share the social and political implications of Holy Wisdom far and wide.

St. John called Christ the *Logos* (in the masculine), or the Word of God. St. Paul named Christ as *Sophia* (in the feminine), or the Wisdom of God. Merton studied the Wisdom literature of the Hebrew Scriptures and was touched by the divine feminine. Holy Wisdom became for him, according to Jim Forest, the union between Creator and creation, the Divine nature, the mercy and tenderness of God.[5] Merton relished passages such as Proverbs 8, where Wisdom plays before God in God's new creation:

Those who love me, I also love, and those who seek me, find me. . . . The Lord begot me, the first born of his ways. . . . From of old, I was poured forth, at the first, before the earth. . . . There was I beside him as his craftsman and I was his delight day by day playing before him all the while, playing on the surface of his earth and I found delight in the sons and daughters of humanity. . . . Happy the one who obeys me and happy those who keep my ways. The one who finds me, finds life, and wins favor from the Lord. The one who misses me, harms himself; all who hate me love death. (Prov. 8:17–36)

As a monk and a poet, Merton fell in love with Holy Wisdom, and it seems, as promised, Wisdom fell in love with him.

This new spiritual insight is striking because it was so rare, even for a monk. For centuries, the institutional male church ignored the feminine dimension of God and cultivated a judgmental, violent, male image of God. Of course, women through the centuries suspected that God was feminine. Most practicing Christian women today know it for sure. But during the Middle Ages, in our hunger for that feminine dimension, Catholics looked to Mary for divine tenderness; she was almost elevated to divine status. Today, the pathology of male domination continues to hurt the global church, tarnishes our understanding of God as nonviolent, and fuels the world's violence.

One wonders specifically if the violent male images of God over the centuries fueled the world's violence, and what might have happened had the Christian churches upheld the feminine side of God as well, if our understanding and search for Holy Wisdom might have disarmed us, led the church to fulfill its vocation of nonviolence, and inspired consistent work for peace. Merton's discovery of the nonviolence of God and his peacemaking vocation blossomed through his simultaneous embrace of Hagia Sophia, which helped him become a person of peace and nonviolence. Pramuk suggests that all of us, individually and collectively as church, need to reclaim the divine feminine, the Wisdom of God, as Merton did, and that Holy Wisdom could help us become, like Merton, people of peace and nonviolence.

What does it mean to recognize Sophia? It happens, Merton writes, when "one awakens strong at the voice of mercy, as if Life his Sister, as if Nature made wise by God's Art and Incarnation were to stand over him and invite him with unutterable sweetness to be awake and to live." Sophia leads to "awakening out of languor and darkness, out of helplessness, out of sleep, newly confronting reality and finding it to be gentleness."[6] Merton continues,

> Gentleness comes to him when he is most helpless and awakens him, refreshed, beginning to be made whole. Love takes him by the hand, and opens to him the doors of another life, another day. ... All that is sweet in her tenderness will speak to him on all sides in everything, without ceasing, and he will never be the same again. He will have awakened not to conquest and dark pleasure but to the impeccable pure simplicity of One consciousness in all and through all: one Wisdom, one Child, one Meaning, one Sister.[7]

This insight into our awakening to gentleness and love, what I've been calling peace and nonviolence, led Merton to his first articulation about the feminine side of God:

> God is at once Father and Mother. As Father, God stands in solitary might surrounded by darkness. As Mother, God's shining is diffused, embracing all God's creatures with merciful tenderness and light. The Diffuse Shining of God is Hagia Sophia. We call her God's "glory." In Sophia, God's power is experienced only as mercy and love.[8]

He continues,

> Sophia is the mercy of God in us. She is the tenderness with which the infinitely mysterious power of pardon turns the darkness of our sins into the light of grace. She is the inexhaustible fountain of kindness, and would almost seem to be, in herself, all mercy. So she does in us a greater work

than that of Creation: the work of new being in grace, the work of pardon, the work of transformation from brightness to brightness *tamquam a Domini Spiritu.* She is in us the yielding and tender counterpart of the power, justice and creative dynamism of the Father.[9]

"Theology is a lifelong conversation with wonder and mystery," Pramuk writes. "To be 'bitten by Merton' is to be initiated into a world of revelation, heightened expectation, and presence."[10] Pramuk reflects on Merton's mystical-prophetic vision of Sophia in light of contemporary Christology, Russian Sophiology, Buddhist Zen practice, John Henry Newman, and Abraham Heschel to show how a new emphasis on Hagia Sophia might help the church and the world as it helped Merton. Pramuk suggests that, just as Hagia Sophia captured Merton's imagination and opened new doors to God and to peace for him, our own attendance to Holy Wisdom will heal us, disarm us, and lead us deeper into God and God's peace.

"The remembrance of Sophia holds significant promise for invigorating Christological and Trinitarian discourse in response to these increasingly fractured, technological, industrialized, and militarized times," Pramuk writes. "Bound up closely with the biblical doctrine of creation and the patristic doctrines of incarnation, divinization, and grace, a Wisdom or Sophia-inspired Christology offers a compelling narrative and metaphysical framework for making old things new again in theological discourse, for reimagining God's vital presence in the natural world, and for reaffirming in boldest dogmatic terms the transcendent dignity of human persons everywhere. . . . Sophia, the theological eros that animated Merton's religious imagination, might be capable of infusing new vitality into ours," Pramuk asserts. "Her voice might awaken in the lives of ordinary Christians, ways both ancient and new, of bringing to birth the love and mercy of Christ in a stricken world."[11] Pramuk's book traces, in his words,

the emergence of Sophia in Merton's life and writings as a Love and a Presence that breaks through into the world, a living symbol and Name through which he encountered the living God and with which he chose, at his poetic and prophetic best, to structure theological discourse. It responds to the question of Merton's mature Christology by advancing the following thesis: it was Sophia, the "unknown and unseen Christ" within all things, who both centered and in many respects catalyzed Merton's theological imagination in a period of tremendous social, political, and religious fragmentation. Drawing intuitively from sources in the Judeo-Christian tradition as well as from non-Christian sources, and inspired especially by the Sophia tradition of Russian Orthodoxy, the Wisdom tradition became Merton's most vivid means of expressing "a living experience of unity in Christ which far transcends all conceptual formulations."[12]

"From the much-discussed epiphany at Fourth and Walnut in March of 1958 to his climactic pilgrimage in Asia," Pramuk notes, "Sophia emerges as a kind of unifying presence and theological wellspring in Merton's life, both centering and catalyzing his outreach to others in friendship, dialogue, and peacemaking." Pramuk suggests that Merton's prophetic turning to the world and the global crises of violence was matched by his turning to the Word of God as the Wisdom of God. Merton's embrace of Sophia was as revolutionary as his prophetic writing; each complemented and enhanced the other. He was able to write wisely about difficult global matters because he had begun literally to worship Holy Wisdom.

Here Pramuk offers an original insight into the explanation of Merton's sudden, dramatic work for peace, and a lesson for us about how we, too, might go forward in the spiritual life, to meet the living God and fulfill our own vocations to be peacemakers.

"It is significant that Merton directs our gaze not to some nameless presence or hidden God-beyond-God," Pramuk asserts, "but to Christ the Wisdom of God, whose light transfigures all creation with love and resurrection hope, and whose presence shines in the face of every human being."[13] "Against the radical commodification of nature, of sex, and of human beings everywhere, Merton interjects the gentle voice of Sophia, 'at once my own being, my own nature, and the Gift of my Creator's

Thought and Art within me.' And a lament: 'We do not hear the soft voice, the gentle voice, the merciful and feminine. We do not hear mercy, or yielding love, or non-resistance. We do not see the Child who is prisoner in all the people.'"[14]

Pramuk concludes that the Sophia tradition implies a way of life—a commitment to prayer, community, simplicity, solitude, artistic and vocational creativity, asceticism—which are all tested means in the Christian tradition for cultivating universal love for humanity and creation. Living with wisdom leads to what monastic spirituality calls "purity of heart, poverty of spirit," what Merton called "the prayerful ground of sanity, of peace."[15] Pramuk writes,

> Sophia is more than a metaphor for the universal presence of God, a kind of anonymous Christology in a feminine key. It is also a kind of real symbol and revealed Name for what Orthodox theology calls "divinization," meaning the fullness of participation in the life of God.[16]

&

> Merton models a way of knowing, centered in Christ, that positively expects to find God's presence "at play" in every corner of reality to which we humbly give ourselves over.[17]

"It is crucial to keep in mind," Pramuk notes, "that the breakthrough of Sophia was not something that simply happened to Merton but was instead the culmination of years of sustained study of patristic and Russian theology, Zen, meditation on Scripture and iconography, and surely more than we can know, untold hours of contemplation in the hills and woods of Gethsemani."[18] He suggests that had Merton lived, he would have advocated Wisdom Christology as "the way forward," in Pramuk's words, into "a vision of all things caught up in the life story of God from the beginning."[19]

"What we must really do," Merton told his brother monks at Gethsemani toward the end of his life, "is live our theology."[20] Pramuk concludes, "To the degree we desire to live in peace with others and in sustainable harmony with 'Mother Earth,' we, too, will have to 'live our theology,' and all such living begins with prayer."[21]

Thomas Merton the peacemaker invites all of us to "live with wisdom," to dedicate ourselves once and for all to the wisdom of peace, the life of peace, and thus the God of peace. In doing so, he tells us that we will be disarmed and healed, live with a new spirit of gentleness, and become peacemakers who publicly denounce violence and war and celebrate love and life to the full. Sophia, for Merton, was "the great stabilizer for peace."[22] Wisdom can be the great stabilizer for all of us—if we are wise enough to choose wisdom!

Living with wisdom, Merton concludes, means "life as communion, life as thanksgiving, life as praise, life as festival, life as glory."[23] What a beautiful description of the life of peace! Living with wisdom means living a nonviolent life. We renounce violence and warmaking, withdraw from the culture of violence and war as much as possible, even like Merton into the woods, and seek the God of peace. From now on, as the book of Proverbs suggests, we have no love for death. We do not serve death; we serve life and live life to the full, and help one and all live life to the full.

I hope that, like Thomas Merton, we will awake to Sophia and discover anew the Wisdom of God within us and among us for the transformation and healing of our lives, and let her guide us on a new path of gentleness, nonviolence, and peace for the healing of our broken church and the warring world. As we awaken to Holy Wisdom and spend our days more and more living with wisdom, Merton promises us that we will enter, in his words, "the realm of mercy, communion and presence."[24] That is the path of the peacemaker. The foolish ignore it, but those who are wise heed that narrow path.

23

The Universe Is My Home

———————

Recently I spent a few days hiking alone in the lush Redwood National Forest in northern California. I went with a purpose in mind—to prepare my mind for trial. I faced the possibility of six months in prison for a protest on Holy Thursday at Creech Air Force Base in Nevada, home to our unmanned drones. But just before I left, word came down. The prosecutor had dropped all charges. I headed for the stately forest just the same.

Little on the planet prepares you for such a sight. The coastal redwoods are the largest trees on the globe. Some reach thirty-five stories tall, some are fifteen hundred years old. I ambled into vast groves of them, my neck craning upward, the sky nearly hidden. Seldom does a sunbeam find its way to the ground.

I had entered upon a sacred world, like a cathedral or a monastery. The mountain air refreshed my senses; the stunning silence and ancient giants put my short life in perspective. Here in the wooded cathedral I found mindfulness-made-easy. Here was Living Peace 101, the Spiritual Life for Dummies. All one has to do is look and breathe. God does the rest.

There the fragrance of God lingers on the air. Said one smitten park ranger, "These groves are God's fingerprints." They seemed to be stretching upward to touch God's face. And it's why several early environmentalists, around the time of the First World War, campaigned to protect this land. If people came here, they rightly figured, folks would find God, and the things that make for war would vanish. The redwoods would teach them peace. That was their hope.

And so I trod gently and opened my senses. And soon tears began—tears of grief for the suffering world, for the destruction of the earth; tears of joy from this immersion in God's grandeur, the sheer height and length and breadth, the wonder of it all. It was as if I had joined a Communion line, a sacred moment in store at the end of the aisle. Except here, time and space evaporate. Everywhere I turned, I found the Creator.

I drove for miles through the redwood groves right along the northern California coast, sat at the edge of cliffs overlooking the Pacific, walked rocky beaches, and came upon several herds of elk. In one field, the elk were sitting down, resting in the tall grass. All you could see were mammoth antlers sticking out above the grass. I breathed deep and for a time shed the memory of the travails of the world.

I took the roundabout route because I had a particular destination in mind: the Monastery of the Redwoods, a community of Cistercian nuns founded in the early 1960s. From Garberville, you drive toward the coast along serpentine roads and enter redwood forests close to the cliffs of Shelter Cove.

Near Whitehorn, you head down another country lane until you see a sign. Soon you'll find yourself in an open field bounded by ancient redwoods on primeval hills. The monastery is in the field. A few modest buildings surround the concrete block chapel, which features a massive wooden altar and a large picture window opening onto a particularly large redwood.

Here Thomas Merton came in May 1968 to offer a workshop on prayer. The place, the women, the solitude, captured his heart. And he got plans under way to move there permanently, to find a hermitage on a nearby cliff. A beautiful dream and an ideal setting. Some months later he visited again on his way to Asia. He hoped to return for Lent the following year, but he died in Bangkok.

The monastery was founded by Mother Myriam Dardenne, a Belgian nun—a legendary woman of wisdom and spirit and charisma. Myriam first met Merton in 1961, when she stopped at the Abbey of Gethsemani on her way to California. Merton recognized right away that she was a visionary, a true leader in the church, and they became friends.

I met Myriam in the late 1990s. She and I and a small group

of activists—including Sr. Helen Prejean, Argentina's Nobel Laureate Adolfo Perez Esquivel, and several of Nelson Mandela's former prison comrades who were now officials in the South African government—made a weeklong retreat together at Gethsemani. I liked Myriam immensely, and we became friends. Here was a lively, charismatic, creative woman full of life and tall tales.

Some were about Merton. During his trip to Asia, she said, he sent her a postcard from Calcutta, saying he had bought an original painting of Jesus from a Calcutta shop and would be sending it to her. Of course, as a cloistered, destitute Cistercian, he never bought anything for anybody, so here was the rarest of occasions. Some weeks passed when news came to her that Merton had died. And grief descended on the small community.

A year and a half later, a delivery truck rumbled onto monastery grounds. And out stepped the driver with a bundle in his hands. Merton's gift had finally arrived.

Her tales drew me in, and I made a mental note: I must visit her at her monastery someday. But the chance never arose. In 2002, while caring for her ill sister in her hometown in Belgium, Myriam herself took ill and died.

At last, though, I had arrived at the beloved monastery. A nun ushered me across the field to a cross at the foot of a redwood. Here was a stone marker and Myriam's ashes. I stood awhile and pondered the deep contradiction: How could a person so intensely alive and full of spirit be gone? Indeed, Myriam makes it easy for me to believe in the resurrection.

Then I got to meet Veronique, the sister who came from Belgium with Myriam over fifty years ago. As a young woman, Veronique left her Belgium home and walked an hour to a Cistercian monastery. When she saw the steeple in the distance, she said to herself: "Ah! My home for the rest of my life!" Little did she think she would spend most of her life in a far-off land called California—nestled among the magnificent redwoods.

The first winter, she said, took a toll. The sisters shivered nights in an abandoned shack in the field. One night the roof caught fire, their only heat that winter, and they scrambled to put it out. Fifty years later, their amenities are still rough and simple, she says. There are a dozen sisters now, and they support themselves by selling honey and offering hospitality. But of course, living simply as they do, they barely make ends meet.

Finally, she took me to see the gift from Merton to Myriam, the painting of Jesus now hanging in the corner of the chapel. I was deeply touched by it. It is plain and simple, the outline of Jesus holding a large cross. The paint is marred by horizontal cracks from the canvass being rolled up for so long. Its simplicity invites compassion and peace.

Nestled in those majestic redwoods, the monastery is a true home of prayer, praise, and peace. The redwoods disarm you and lead you unwittingly to the Creator, the God of peace. This is what creation will do if we let creation teach us. If we live disconnected from the earth and the beauty of creation—worse, if we destroy creation—we will never meet the Creator, the God of peace. The Grand Canyon, Yosemite, Arches, and Zion National Parks; any beach; any mountain; all their creatures—they all point back to a loving Creator.

"Here there is an authentic atmosphere of prayer," Merton told the nuns of the redwoods. "Enjoy this. Drink it all in. Everything—the redwood forests, the sea, the sky, the wave, the birds, the sea lions. It is in all this that you will find your answers. Here is where everything connects."[1]

Everything connects! Here is one of the classic teachings of Thomas Merton. While he was writing about peace and nonviolence under the Gospel teaching, "Blessed are the meek," he was already living out the promised blessing: "They shall inherit the earth." Merton learned through his monastic life of nonviolence to make peace with creation. In the 1950s he was the first monk allowed to wander the thousands of acres on their premises. He became the monastery's forester, spent hours in the fire watchtower, and personally planted thousands of trees. By the time he was living alone in the woods, he knew the name of every pair of birds, every tree and flower, and every creature that made up his little "ecology of peace."

Many passages in his writings celebrate his connection with creation. One of my favorites is from "Rain and the Rhinoceros," where Merton ponders "the festival of rain." The passage itself opens a window into Merton's spiritual life—he is part of nature, one with nature:

At the moment the rain is still free, and I am in it. I celebrate its gratuity and its meaninglessness. It fills the woods with an immense and confused sound. It covers the flat roof of the cabin and its porch with insistent and controlled rhythms. And I listen, because it reminds me again and again that the whole world runs by rhythms I have not yet learned to recognize, rhythms that are not those of the engineer.

I came up here from the monastery last night, sloshing through the cornfield, said Vespers, and put some oatmeal on the Coleman stove for supper. It boiled over while I was listening to the rain, and toasting a piece of bread at the log fire. The night became very dark. The rain surrounded the whole cabin with its enormous virginal myth, a whole world of meaning, of secrecy, of silence, of rumor. Think of it: all that speech pouring down, selling nothing, judging nobody, drenching the thick mulch of dead leaves, soaking the trees, filling the gullies and crannies of the wood with water, washing out the places where men have stripped the hillside! What a thing it is to sit absolutely alone, in the forest, at night, cherished by this wonderful unintelligible, perfectly innocent speech, the most comforting speech in the world, the talk that rain makes by itself all over the ridges, and the talk of the watercourses everywhere in the hollows! Nobody started it, nobody is going to stop it. It will talk as long as it wants, this rain. As long as it talks I am going to listen.[2]

Before we knew of catastrophic climate change, the depletion of the ozone layer, the rise in global temperature and sea levels, the Sixth Extinction of hundreds of thousands of creatures, the disappearance of drinking water, and destructive hurricanes, droughts, tornadoes, and wildfires, before most of us realized the obvious priority of care for the earth, Merton devoted his life to creation. Like St. Francis and Mahatma Gandhi, he made himself right with the ecology, with creatures and creation. He embodies the connection between the spiritual life of peace and oneness with creation. In doing so, his life teaches us that we cannot be peacemakers without making peace first with the earth—all her creatures, indeed, the entire universe.

"The universe is my home," Merton learned. Here's his journal entry for March 2, 1965:

> One thing the hermitage is making me see is that the universe is my home and I am nothing if not part of it. Destruction of the self that seems to stand outside the universe. Get free from the illusion of solipsism. Only as part of the world's fabric and dynamism can I find my true being in God, who has willed me to exist in the world. This, I discover here in the hermitage, not mentally only but in depth and wholeness, especially, for instance, in the ability to sleep. At the monastery, frogs kept me awake. There are frogs here but they do not keep me awake. They are a comfort, an extension of my own being. Now the hum of the electric meter near my bed is nothing, though in the monastery it would have been intolerable. So there is an acceptance of nature and even of technology in my true habitat. I do not have to work the thing out *theoretically*. It is working itself out in practice in a way that does not need to be explained or justified.[3]

One good day, April 13, 1963, he felt so at one with the nature around him, he could barely pray the psalms. Such days led him to reflect on our oneness with creation.

> When was there ever such a morning as yesterday? Cold at first, the hermitage dark in the moonlight, a fire in the grate (and how beautifully firelight shines through the lattice-blocks and all through the house at night!). Then the sunrise, enormous yolk of energy spreading and spreading as if to take over the sky. After that the ceremonies of the birds feeding in the dewy grass, and the meadowlark feeding and singing. Then the quiet, totally silent, day, warm mid-morning under the climbing sun. It was hard to say psalms: one's attention was totally absorbed by the great arc of the sky and the trees and hills and grass and all things in them. How absolutely true, and how central a truth, that we are purely and simply *part of nature*, though we are the part which recognizes God. It is not Christian-

ity, indeed, but post-Cartesian technologism that separates
humanity from the world and makes it a kind of little god
in his own right, and his clear ideas; all by himself. We have
to be humbly and realistically what we are, and the denial
of it results only in the madness and cruelties of Nazism,
or of the people who are sick with junk and drugs. So that
was one good day.[4]

The spiritual life of peace requires living humbly, mindfully,
intentionally aware of our oneness with creation. If we live
apart from nature, if we forget that we are one with creation,
we turn to violence and war, and end up, in Merton's estimation,
like the Nazis! Here's a similar journal entry, one year later on
April 23, 1964, where once again he exults in the "heavenliness
of creation":

> I live in a mixture of heavenliness and anguish. Sometimes
> I suddenly see "heavenliness." For instance, in the pure,
> pure white of the mature dogwood blossoms against the
> dark evergreens in the cloudy garden. "Heavenliness" too
> of the song of the unknown bird that is perhaps here for
> only one or two days, passing through. A lively deep simple
> song. Pure, no pathos, no statement, no desire, just pure
> heavenly sound. I am seized by this heavenliness as if I
> were a child, a child mind I have never done anything to
> deserve, and which is my own part in the heavenly spring.
> This is not of this world nor is it of my own making. It is
> born partly of physical anguish which is really not deep,
> though. The anguish goes so quickly. I have a sense that
> this underlying heavenliness is the real nature of things.
> Not their nature, but the deeper truth that they are a gift
> of love and of freedom, and that this is their true reality.[5]

For Merton, authentic worship of God and universal nonviolent love for humanity went hand in hand with stewardship
toward creatures and creation, indeed, celebrating the beauty of
creation. We hear this in one of Merton's most important prayers,
"A Prayer to God the Father on the Vigil of Pentecost," in which
he placed his life and soul within the physical reality of creation:

Today, Father, this blue sky lauds you. The delicate green and orange flowers of the tulip poplar tree praise you. The distant blue hills praise you, together with the sweet-smelling air that is full of brilliant light. The bickering flycatchers praise you with the lowing cattle and the quails that whistle over there. I too, Father, praise you, with all these my brothers and sisters, and they give voice to my own heart and to my own silence. We are all one silence, and a diversity of voices.

You have made us together, you have made us one and many, you have placed me here in the midst as witness, as awareness, and as joy. Here I am. In me the world is present and you are present. I am a link in the chain of light and of presence. You have made me a kind of center, but a center that is nowhere. And yet also I am "here," let us say I am "here" under these trees, not others.

If I have any choice to make, it is to live here and perhaps die here. But in any case it is not the living or the dying that matter, but speaking your name with confidence in this light, in this unvisited place: to speak your name of "father" just by being here as "son" in the Spirit and the Light which you have given, and which are no unearthly light but simply this plain June day, with its shining fields, its tulip tree, the pines, the woods, the clouds, and the flowers everywhere.

To be here with the silence of Sonship in my heart is to be a center in which all things converge upon you. That is surely enough of the time being.

Therefore, Father, I beg you to keep me in this silence so that I may learn from it the word of your peace and the word of your mercy and the word of your gentleness to the world: and that through me perhaps your word of peace may make itself heard where it has not been possible for anyone to hear it for a long time.

To study truth here and learn here to suffer for truth. The Light itself, and the contentment and the Spirit, these are enough. Amen.[6]

Notice how his prayer to God flows from his mindful awareness of the beautiful creation around him, and this leads him to an awareness of his true self, his ultimate identity—as the beloved Son of God. For me, this remains the core definition of a peacemaker: "Blessed are the peacemakers; they shall be called the sons and daughters of the God of peace." There in the silence of creation, he begged to hear God's word of peace, mercy, and gentleness that he might share God's word with the world. There in the beauty and peace of creation, he discovered again his vocation.

That's what happens to all of us when we claim our oneness with creation, when we make peace with the earth. We discover who we are and who we are called to be.

Years earlier, in *New Seeds of Contemplation*, Merton explored the connection between our awareness of creation and our true identities. He wrote,

> A tree gives glory to God by being a tree. For in being what God means it to be it is obeying God. It "consents," so to speak, to God's creative love. . . . The more a tree is like itself, the more it is like God. No two created beings are exactly alike. This particular tree will give glory to God by spreading out its roots in the earth and raising its branches into the air and the light in a way that no other tree before or after it ever did or will do. . . .
>
> The forms and individual characters of living and growing things, or inanimate beings, of animals and flowers and all nature, constitute their holiness in the sight of God. . . . The special clumsy beauty of this particular clot on this April day in this field under these clouds is a holiness consecrated to God by God's own creative wisdom and it declares the glory of God. The pale flowers of the dogwood outside this window are saints. The little yellow flowers that nobody notices on the edge of that road are saints looking up into the face of God. The lakes hidden among the hills are saints, and the sea too is a saint who praises God without interruption in her majestic dance. The great, gashed, half-naked mountain is another of God's saints. There is no other like him. He is alone in his own character; nothing else in the world ever did or ever will imitate God in quite the same way. That is his sanctity.

But what about you? What about me? Unlike the animals and the trees, it is not enough for us to be what our nature intends. It is not enough for us to be individual men and women. For us, holiness is more than humanity. For me to be a saint means to be myself. Therefore the problem of sanctity and salvation is in fact the problem of finding out who I am and of discovering my true self. Trees and animals have no problem. God makes them what they are without consulting them, and they are perfectly satisfied. With us it is different. God leaves us free to be whatever we like. We can be ourselves or not, as we please. We are at liberty to be real, or to be unreal. We may be true or false, the choice is ours. . . . Our vocation is not simply to be, but to work together with God in the creation of our own life, our own identity, our own destiny. We are free beings and sons and daughters of God.[7]

Creation, for Thomas Merton, teaches us about the God of peace, but also about ourselves. It helps us discover our true identities as God's sons and daughters. This is another key lesson from the life of Thomas Merton.

"To be alone by being part of the universe—fitting in completely to an environment of woods and silence and peace," Merton wrote in his journal. "Everything you do becomes a unity and a prayer. Unity within and without. Unity with all living things—without effort or contention. My silence is part of the whole world's silence and builds the temple of God without the noise of hammers."[8]

My visit to the Monastery of the Redwoods ended too soon, but how grateful I am for those days. The redwoods, tall and ancient, make a mockery of our sense of time. Their grandeur shrinks our self-importance. And by their ponderous silence, they refresh and renew and show us what peace looks and feels like. And the sisters maintain a living prayer, and model the Christian life of peace. They are peacemakers, daughters of the God of peace. I know I will return.

I find it essential to retreat periodically to monasteries and such parks. For me, there is no other way to stay involved in the long haul for justice and peace. The glories of nature restore my soul, ease my breathing, sturdy me for the road ahead. It is pristine, undisturbed nature—and the peaceful community of prayer—that reminds us that our life journeys are intended for peace, that the road ahead is marked by peace, that every day can be an opportunity to live and breathe in the peace of creation and hear God's word of peace and welcome Christ's peace.

Creation helps us fulfill our vocations to be the sons and daughters of the God of peace—peacemakers. As peacemakers, like Merton, from now on, the universe is our home. We, too, know that we are one with creation, and do our best to protect it.

The Prayer of Union
and Communion

By the time Merton entered the monastery in 1941 at age twenty-six, he had already lived several lifetimes. He had seen up close the traps, failures, illusions, and violence of the world. He was ready for "God Alone," as the sign over the entranceway to Gethsemani read. By all accounts, he was a man full of life, wit, and warmth, with a towering intellectual curiosity. But from entrance day onward, he became, first and foremost, a man of steadfast prayer. Prayer was his life, a way of life that sought God alone. As a writer, he documented his monastic life, and the theological, spiritual, and intellectual discoveries that sprang from long hours of silence, solitude, Bible study, community liturgy, and openness to God.

Can we too seek "God alone"? Can we seek the God of peace with full attention and concentration, no matter what our state of life? If we want to discover peace and open up to the God of peace as Merton did, we might try to give our lives to "God Alone." That means, at some fundamental level, in our daily prayer, solitude, and sacramental life, we surrender ourselves, our minds, our hearts, our will, and our lives to the God of peace in the fullness of love and freedom. Like Merton, we may discover that the more we give ourselves unconditionally to God, the more we become our true selves and, at the same time, become one with all humanity, all creatures, and all creation, in welcoming God's reign of peace on earth. The pursuit of the God of peace in a lifelong relationship will transform us into peacemakers, at one with humanity and creation, sent to disarm the world. This is a good thing, worthy of our attention, concentration, and surrender!

"Our real journey in life is interior," Merton wrote his friends from Asia in the fall of 1968. "It is a matter of growth, deepening, and of an ever greater surrender to the creative action of love and grace in our hearts."[1] As Merton continued to go deeper into the life of prayer and openness to God, as he explored his own interior life, he distinguished between the false self and true self. Creation, prayer, community, friends, and the struggle for justice and peace helped him become his true self. Over time, he realized that his true self was to be the beloved son of the God of peace. This vocation, he knew, was the vocation of every human being—each one of us is a beloved son or daughter of the God of peace, a peacemaker sent to help abolish war and injustice and live the gift of life to the full, with respect for one another and creation.

The interior journey toward our true selves, into our true identities as sons and daughters of the God of peace, leads us to union with the God of peace. At the same time, it opens a new awareness of our oneness with every human being as our sister or brother, even our unity with all creatures and all creation. Merton's conscious life shows us how we, too, can live a life of peace through prayer and learn to make peace with ourselves, with God, with humanity and with all creation. Living in peace, he shows, means living in union with the God of peace and full communion with humanity and creation.

For all his writings about prayer, he hardly ever described his own experience. Toward the end of his life, on January 2, 1966, he wrote a long, revealing description of his daily spiritual practice to his friend and Sufi scholar Abdul Aziz, who had asked about Merton's private prayer. It gives us a rare glimpse into the inner life of a peacemaker.

Strictly speaking, I have a very simple way of prayer. It is centered entirely on attention to the presence of God and to His will and His love. That is to say that it is centered on faith by which alone we can know the presence of God. One might say this gives my meditation the character described by the Prophet as "being before God as if you saw Him." Yet it does not mean imagining anything or conceiving a precise image of God, for to my mind this would be a kind of idolatry. On the contrary, it is a matter of adoring God as invisible and infinitely beyond our comprehension, and realizing God as all. . . . There is in my heart this great thirst to recognize totally the nothingness of all that is not God. My prayer is then a kind of praise rising up out of the center of Nothing and Silence. If I am still present "myself" this I recognize as an obstacle about which I can do nothing unless God Himself removes the obstacle. If God wills God can then make the Nothingness into a total clarity. If God does not will, then the Nothingness seems to itself to be an object and remains an obstacle. Such is my ordinary way of prayer, or meditation. It is not "thinking about" anything, but a direct seeking of the Face of the Invisible, which cannot be found unless we become lost in God who is Invisible.[2]

This letter reveals his serious openness to the Mystery of God, either as dwelling in the peaceful presence of God, or the peaceful absence of God, which he called "The Void." In either case, he shows up and waits upon God. This steadfast, earnest practice is the first stage in the life of peace, for it puts aside our personal illusions and ego mindlessness, as well as every aspect of the culture of war and injustice, to center our attention on the God of peace in the context of creation's peace and our body's own peace, in its breath. In this contemplative prayer, our idols fall away. Everything falls away—ego, money, ambition, attachment, our nation, its military might, and its false security. The culture of violence and war falls to the side, and we enter the truth of reality. As we sit in the present moment, *everything connects*! As peacemakers who learn from Thomas Merton, we, too, seek the God of peace with dedication, discipline, radical openness, and awareness of our union with God. In doing so, we enter the fullness of life in communion with all humanity and creation.

In his last years, Merton wrote more about universal love and peace for all human beings as the fruit of the spiritual life, as a sign of our faith, and as the practice of authentic Christianity. Universal nonviolent love was the solution to the world's problems, the flip side of our prophetic truth-telling, the heart of our peacemaking. In *Seeds of Destruction* he warned of the dangers of failing at universal love:

> Where there is a deep, simple, all-embracing love of humanity, of the created world of living and inanimate things, then there will be respect for life, for freedom, for truth, for justice and there will be humble love of God. But where there is no love of humanity, no love of life, then make all the laws you want, all the edicts and treaties, issue all the anathemas, set up all the safeguards and inspections, fill the air with spying satellites, and hang cameras on the moon. As long as you see your fellow human beings essentially to be feared, mistrusted, hated, and destroyed, there cannot be peace on earth.[3]

As Merton tried to practice universal love and peace, he felt a desire to embody the oneness of the world in himself, beginning with recovering the unity of the churches. Here's his journal entry from April 28, 1957:

> If I can unite in myself the thought and the devotion of Eastern and Western Christendom, the Greek and the Latin Fathers, the Russian with the Spanish mystics, I can prepare in myself the reunion of divided Christians. From that secret and unspoken unity in myself can eventually come a visible and manifest unity of all Christians. If we want to bring together what is divided, we cannot do so by imposing one division upon the other. If we do this, the union is not Christian. It is political and doomed to further conflict. We must contain all the divided worlds in ourselves and transcend them in Christ.[4]

Like Merton, we, too, can desire to embody universal nonviolent love, to unite humanity in ourselves. We, too, can model the unity we seek for others. We can try to unite in ourselves all the peoples of the world—including Iraq, Afghanistan, Palestine, Cuba, Sudan, and Congo; all the races, religions, and cultures of the world. Like Merton, in particular, we can embody a new kind of interfaith nonviolence, with respect toward all religions, and friendship toward one and all. This life of inner unity that seeks global unity can even seek unity with all creatures and creation.

Merton's long interior journey to the God of peace and his true self led him to universal love for humanity and oneness with creation. His journey, like that of the saints and other mystics, teaches us that the pursuit of universal nonviolent love, universal peace, universal compassion, and universal nonviolence is the highest, transcendent dimension of the spiritual life. Every religious search that continues deeper and deeper leads to this transcendent plane of universal love, peace, compassion, and nonviolence.

Oddly enough, such universal love and peace are rarely espoused by "professional" religious people and leaders, and often are scoffed at and dismissed. What should be the highest goal of every church and every Christian is rarely even recognized as a good. Instead, that transcendent spiritual level of universal love and peace is most often found on the margins among marginal people—the poor, the artist, the activist, and the child.

Speaking at the first Spiritual Summit Conference in Calcutta, India, just weeks before his death, Merton expressed his hope that we can plumb the depths of love and peace and discover that universal love and peace, the hidden ground of being, which unite us as sisters and brothers. "In all the great world religions there are a few individuals and communities who dedicate themselves in a special way to living out the full consequences and implications of what they believe," he began his speech.[5] He spoke of the "inner transformation" that monastics seek, "a deepening of consciousness toward an eventual breakthrough and discovery of a transcendent dimension of life beyond that of the ordinary empirical self and of ethical and pious observance."[6] Though he was speaking about the efforts of monastics to reach the spiritual heights and share those realizations with one another, his insights, I submit, can be broadened to include all religions, all cultures, and all peoples. He continued,

I am convinced that communication in depth, across the lines that have hitherto divided religious and monastic traditions, is now not only possible and desirable, but more important for the destinies of twentieth-century humanity. . . . True communication on the deepest level is more than a simple sharing of ideas, of conceptual knowledge, or formulated truth. The kind of communication that is necessary on this deep level must also be "communion" beyond the level of words, a communion in authentic experience which is shared not only on a "preverbal" level but also on a "postverbal" level. The "preverbal" level is that of the unspoken and indefinable "preparation," "the predisposition" of mind and heart. . . . The "postverbal" level will then, at least ideally, be that on which they both meet beyond their own words and their own understanding in the silence of an ultimate experience which might conceivably not have occurred if they had not met and spoken. This I would call "communion." I think it is something that the deepest ground of our being cries out for, and it is something for which a lifetime of striving would not be enough.[7]

He urged monks to "keep alive the contemplative experience and to keep the way open for modern technological humanity to recover the integrity of his own inner depths." That is the task of every peacemaker:

It is important that this element of depth and integrity—this element of inner transcendent freedom—be kept intact as we grow toward the full maturity of universal humanity. We are witnessing the growth of a truly universal consciousness of transcendent freedom and vision, or it may simply be a vast blur of mechanized triviality and ethical cliché.[8]

In a different, more informal talk on monasticism in Calcutta, he concluded:

The deepest level of communication is not communication but communion. It is wordless. It is beyond words, and it is beyond speech, and it is beyond concept. Not that we discover a new unity. We discover an older unity. My dear brothers and sisters, we are already one. But we imagine that we are not. What we have to recover is our original unity. What we have to be is what we are.[9]

At the end of the conference, Merton offered a beautiful closing prayer, that we might grow in universal nonviolent love for one another, into a deeper awareness of each other as sister and brother, and a greater union with God and creation. It is a prayer that we might become who we already are—sons and daughters of the God of peace; sisters and brothers of one another; instruments of God's love, peace, and compassion.

> Oh God, we are one with You. You have made us one with You. You have taught us that if we are open to one another, You dwell in us. Help us to preserve this openness and to fight for it with all our hearts. Help us to realize that there can be no understanding where there is mutual rejection. Oh God, in accepting one another wholeheartedly, fully, completely, we accept You, and we thank You, and we adore You, and we love You with our whole being, because our being is in Your being, our spirit is rooted in Your spirit. Fill us then with love, and let us be bound together with love as we go our diverse ways, united in this one spirit which makes You present in the world, and which makes You witness to the ultimate reality that is love. Love has overcome. Love is victorious. Amen.[10]

As peacemakers, we want to live in union with the God of peace, and with all humanity and all creation. We grieve the violence, wars, and destruction; rejoice in the fullness of life; pray for the coming of God's reign of peace on earth; and join the nonviolent movements for justice and disarmament. But ultimately, like Merton, we quietly seek that transcendent dimension of communion with God and every human being. We want to be who we were created to be, to become who we already are—the sons and daughters of the God of peace, peacemakers to our poor world.

Everything Is Emptiness
and Everything Is Compassion

———————

Thomas Merton was a destroyed person.

By that, I mean he was not just burnt out, but crushed by the world, by the struggle for justice and peace, by life itself, as millions, perhaps billions of us, are crushed at some point in our lives.

"I walk from region to region of my soul and discover that I am a bombed city," he once wrote in his journal. "Although I am ruined," he wrote at the end of that particular passage, "I am far better off than I have ever been in my life. My ruin is my fortune."[1]

As a follower of the nonviolent Jesus, Thomas Merton walked the way of the cross and shared in Jesus's cross. As a faithful disciple, he lived a long-suffering love, which was fruitful and redemptive, which gave his writings and witness power. Yet his life was not easy, as he occasionally hinted.

Merton knew the world well, having traveled so much, met so many, and befriended so many correspondents. He gave up everything when he entered the Trappist monastery of Gethsemani, on December 10, 1941, as all monks do. But because he was so gifted, because he was such a brilliant writer, a towering intellectual, an unparalleled genius, he never quite fit in, try as he might, and since he was determined to stay, he was ensured a long, quiet suffering. He wrote as much in *The Sign of Jonas*, saying he felt like a duck in a chicken coop.

"I believe my vocation is essentially that of a pilgrim and an exile in life," Merton wrote to a friend in 1962, "that I have no proper place in this world but that for that reason I am in some sense to be the friend and brother of people everywhere, especially those who are exiles and pilgrims like myself."[2]

This long-suffering life is hard to grasp from his writings. The Trappist life is very hard, as anyone who visits monasteries knows. Monks vow among other things to stay put, and as the years pass, drudgery sets in. If you don't get along with your abbot, life can be hell. Merton suffered terribly for many years under Abbot Fox, as all the biographies and journals disclose, even though, of course, Abbot Fox was a great help to Merton and a very good man. Merton recognized the sheer authoritarianism of church leaders, including most bishops, priests, and members of the Roman curia. He lamented the idolatry of hierarchy, the clinical narcissism of many churchmen, and the failures of the institutional church to advocate for peace and nonviolence, even as Vatican II began.

As Merton grew in consciousness about war and injustice, and committed himself to peace and nonviolence, he was bound to suffer even more. He felt the horrors of racism, war, poverty, nuclear weapons, the Vietnam War, and environmental destruction and grieved the lack of concern by most priests, monks, and lay Catholics. He poured out his sweat and blood in those passionate essays and books on peace and social issues, only to have them banned by pro-war monks and bishops or dismissed by most Catholics. Then he discovered how hard it was to live alone in a hermitage in the woods. You have to face your raw self every day—morning, noon, and night. On top of this, we note that every great writer has to dig deep within to unearth truth, a path of suffering, which is why so many brilliant writers end up as alcoholics, drug addicts, or worse.

Then in March 1966, while in a Louisville hospital for back surgery, Merton fell wildly in love with a wonderful, beautiful, lively young student nurse. As his journals attest he seriously contemplated leaving the monastery and religious life to marry her, but in the end, after several months, he broke it off and remained a monk and a hermit. That decision nearly killed him all over again. That is why I say he was a destroyed person. His life was a long-suffering, a long loneliness. Merton carried the cross.

Merton would probably disagree with this summary; indeed, he never put it that way. He was well aware of the great suffering in the world, from the bombed children of Vietnam to the rural poor of Kentucky. He knew how privileged he was, how rich the monastery had become, how comfortably he lived, whether in the monastery or in the hermitage, even when he had no heat or plumbing.

Through all this, Merton remained steadfast. He continued his practice, kept on praying and meditating, stayed mindful and nonviolent, remained centered in Christ and sought the God of peace. His fidelity led him in the end to a new kind of peace, through the other side of the cross to the life of boundless compassion.

It happened in Ceylon, now Sri Lanka, one week before he died.

The seven volumes of Thomas Merton's journals are an unparalleled daily record of a Christian struggling to live the life of faith and prayer, to remain faithful to the God of peace and the monastic life, to seek truth and speak out on behalf of justice and peace, to practice and teach the nonviolence of Jesus, and to remain fresh, true, open, honest, and hopeful. In the early years we find passages where he glories in the monastic life and the grounds, even as he obsesses about joining the Carthusians or seeking out some more perfect life of prayer and solitude. After his revelation at the corner of Fourth and Walnut, when he remembers that he loves everyone, he turns to address the world and its violence, only to be rebuffed and rejected time and time again. Though the hermitage leads him to new joy and a new lease on life, he continues to resent his abbot, and he falls into depression over the authoritarian treatment he receives. By 1966 he was hurt, lonely, and vulnerable. Remember—in the years after Vatican II, tens of thousands of priests around the country and the world left the priesthood. Everything was coming apart. Falling madly in love was an almost normal, albeit unforeseen, next step. Choosing to remain a monk and a hermit only compounded his pain. But 1968 began with the election of a new abbot, an entirely different kind of person, one of Merton's former students, who accepted the job especially so that he could help Merton continue his universal mission to the church and the world. He gave Merton permission to travel—to California, New Mexico, and Alaska, even to explore remote places where they might start a small community of hermits, still connected to Gethsemani. He also gave Merton permission to attend the Bangkok conference, and more—to explore monastic and Buddhist sites in India and Sri Lanka, and afterward, in Indonesia and Japan, perhaps even to travel as a pilgrim for several years.

Merton's turmoil could not subside because 1968 was, in his words, "a brute of a year"—the Tet Offensive, the assassinations of Martin Luther King Jr. and Robert Kennedy, the arrest of Daniel Berrigan and the Catonsville Nine, the police brutality at the Democratic convention in Chicago, and the election of Richard Nixon. Merton spends the summer publishing a poetry magazine, reading up on Asia, and preparing for his long pilgrimage. He flies off to Chicago, New Mexico, California, Alaska, and finally Asia—to Bangkok, New Delhi, Calcutta, Colombo, Singapore, and back to Bangkok. The trip is exhilarating, exhausting, and overwhelming. Merton reads, writes, and talks as if to make up for twenty-seven years behind the monastic walls. He has three memorable encounters with the Dalai Lama, and finds in him not only a peer but a new friend.

But nothing prepares him for the revelation of Polonnaruwa, the Buddhist shrine with the towering stone-carved statues of Buddha reclining and seated, and Ananda his disciple standing tall with a half-smile. The sleeping, dying Buddha lying on his side is perfectly peaceful. Ananda stands next to him in perfect peace. Nothing prepares us, his readers, for this spiritual experience either.

When I first read this passage in 1982 I thought that moment in Polonnaruwa was providential. It seemed to me the finger of God led Merton from France to Britain to America to the monastery of Gethsemani to the hermitage to New Mexico, California, and Alaska, and finally to India and Sri Lanka and Polonnaruwa. It was this moment, not his speech in Bangkok a week later, two hours before his accidental death, that was the climax of his life.

Merton died one week after the greatest spiritual experience of his life. I believe that what happened to Merton at Polonnaruwa was meant for all of us, that the God of peace touched Merton in this transfiguration moment, and that his spiritual experience and the lessons he learned are critically important for all those who walk the path of peace, who follow the nonviolent Jesus, who try to fulfill their vocations as peacemakers.

Here's the full account, written in Colombo, Ceylon, four days later, on December 4, 1968. I invite readers to undergo the experience with Merton, even if you have read this passage many times, and to experience the moment with him, to be disarmed and transformed with him, so that together we can hear his wisdom and go forth as peacemakers:

> I am able to approach the Buddhas barefoot and undisturbed, my feet in wet grass, wet sand. Then the silence of the extraordinary faces. The great smiles. Huge and yet subtle. Filled with every possibility, questioning nothing, knowing everything, rejecting nothing, the peace not of emotional resignation but of Madhyamika [the "middle path" school of Buddhism], of sunyata [emptiness, the Void, or in the Dalai Lama's definition, "the knowledge of the ultimate reality of all objects"], that has seen through every question without trying to discredit anyone or anything—without refutation—without establishing some other argument. For the doctrinaire, the mind that needs well-established positions, such peace, such silence, can be frightening. I was knocked over with a rush of relief and thankfulness at the obvious clarity of the figures, the clarity and fluidity of shape and line, the design of the monumental bodies composed into the rock shape and landscape, figure, rock and tree. And the sweep of bare rock sloping away on the other side of the hollow, where you can go back and see different aspects of the figures.
>
> Looking at these figures I was suddenly, almost forcibly, jerked clean out of the habitual, half-tied vision of things, and an inner clearness, clarity, as if exploding from the rocks themselves became evident and obvious. The queer evidence of the reclining figure, the smile, the sad smile of Ananda standing with arms folded (much more "impera-

tive" than Da Vinci's Mona Lisa because completely simple and straightforward).

The thing about all this is that there is no puzzle, no problem, and really no "mystery." All problems are resolved and everything is clear, simply because what matters is clear. The rock, all matter, all life, is charged with dharmakaya [a Sanskrit term for "the cosmical body of the Buddha, the essence of all beings"].

Everything is emptiness and everything is compassion.

I don't know when in my life I have ever had such a sense of beauty and spiritual validity running together in one aesthetic illumination. Surely with Mahabalipuram and Polonnaruwa, my Asian pilgrimage has come clear and purified itself. I mean, I know and have seen what I was obscurely looking for.[3]

Everything is emptiness and everything is compassion.

Is this the final lesson from our peacemaking teacher, Thomas Merton? Perhaps. It is certainly one peacemakers need to hear, ponder, learn, and live.

If we follow the nonviolent Jesus, practice creative nonviolence, seek the God of peace in daily meditation, claim our true identities as sons and daughters of the God of peace, and speak out publicly for God's reign of peace in a world of permanent war, we will receive in turn, not praise and honor, but resentment, rejection, harassment, persecution, or worse. We might even suffer betrayal, abandonment, arrest, torture, and execution like the nonviolent Jesus. Yes, if we walk in the footsteps of the nonviolent Jesus, we may well suffer the same consequences as he did. That is why Jesus speaks over and over again of the cross.

As I read the Gospels, that seems to be the overriding message to the disciples, to the group he is trying to form into nonviolent peacemakers—"Follow me, go forth with the good news of peace, announce God's reign of nonviolence, expel the demons of violence and empire, but remember, I am sending you as lambs into the midst of wolves. You will be rejected, and some of you will be killed, so if you want to follow me, prepare now to take up the cross." Jesus trains his disciples to respond with loving nonviolence to rejection and persecution from the culture of war. He doesn't train them to be "successful" or "effective." He sends them out as missionaries of nonviolence into the culture of violence.

Thomas Merton fulfilled that mission of gospel nonviolence, which is to say, he carried the cross throughout his life, though it's hard to see on the surface. He faced rejection, resentment, harassment, and persecution, and responded with nonviolent love, while continuing to speak the truth and seek the God of peace. His turn to Buddhist mindfulness and the present moment of peace helped him to respond ever more nonviolently, to go forward and maintain his peace, even as the institutional church and some of his own brother monks rejected Jesus's way of nonviolence.

At Polonnaruwa, Merton was transfigured and tasted the other side of the cross. That is one way to understand his breathtaking statement, "Everything is emptiness and everything is compassion." This is the feeling, truth, and wisdom of the nonviolent Jesus as he undergoes the consequences of his public peacemaking, as he suffers abandonment, arrest, torture, and execution. Jesus lets go completely and empties himself in perfect universal, nonviolent love. St. Paul calls it *kenosis*, self-emptying love into perfect compassion and nonviolence (Phil. 2). It led to resurrection peace and joy. Jesus lived, suffered, and died in perfect nonviolence, as Gandhi said, letting go of every trace of resentment, hurt, bitterness, vengeance, or retaliation. He entered the present moment of peace in total emptiness into perfect compassion. Resurrection is the inevitable outcome of perfect nonviolence. In this new state, there is not a trace of violence, not a trace of death itself, and so the risen Jesus offers us a new gift of peace.

Everything is emptiness and everything is compassion.

We do not need to travel to Sri Lanka to see for ourselves the beautiful Buddhist statues at Polonnaruwa. We have Merton's journal, his own record of his spiritual breakthrough. The nonviolent Jesus, the Buddha, and Thomas Merton the peacemaker invite us to live from now on in the present moment of perfect peace—in the *kenosis*, the emptiness, the self-emptying love of Christ—into perfect compassion for ourselves, all people, and all creation. That means, no matter what obstacles we face, including rejection, harassment, persecution, or worse, we do not cling to the hurt; we let go of the pain and respond with nonviolence, remaining in the present moment of peace. We move deeper into infinite compassion.

"In our resistance to humankind's destruction, we need to live and act in that spirit of ultimate perfect emptiness and compassion if we are to experience a way of transformation," Merton's friend Jim Douglass writes in light of Merton's experience at Polonnaruwa.[4] Douglass continues,

> Our own sin can, through a responsible insight, be converted into an undiscovered energy for change. We are all one, and the person responsible for global evils, as confirmed by our own radical insight into consciousness, is not somewhere out there but right here. . . . We seldom experience the primary truth: the responsibility of each for all through the recognition of one's own sin as fundamental to the most destructive violence and evil, as seen in widening circles from one's own immediate situation extending outward to the entire world. Without denying that evil has many external agents in the world, its ultimate source and responsibility comes home with startling clarity when we are finally humbled enough by reality to see simply and clearly—that as we are, so is the world. At that point, we become open to Merton's way of transformation, as experienced in his encounter with the Buddhas, where everything is emptiness and everything is compassion. We begin then to walk on that transforming way of ultimate perfect emptiness and compassion.[5]

The Dalai Lama, too, speaks of Merton's emphasis on compassion as the key to transformation. A few years ago, he wrote an editorial in *The New York Times* to stress the importance of compassion:

> A main point in my discussion with Merton was how central compassion was to the message of both Christianity and Buddhism. In my readings of the New Testament, I find myself inspired by Jesus' acts of compassion. His miracle

of the loaves and fishes, his healings and his teachings are all motivated by the desire to relieve suffering. I'm a firm believer in the power of personal contact to bridge differences, so I've long been drawn to dialogues with people of other religious outlooks. The focus on compassion that Merton and I observed in our two religions strikes me as a strong unifying thread among all the major faiths. And these days we need to highlight what unifies us.[6]

For the peacemaker, everything is emptiness and everything is compassion. There is no more rush, no more violence, no more ambition, no more fear, no more resentment, no more bitterness, no more death. We have let go of all that, transcending the culture of violence and war and entering God's reign of peace, and so we have set out on a new course of transforming nonviolence and boundless compassion. This is what Merton learned from Buddhism in his fidelity to the risen Christ and realized experientially one week before he died. This is how we are to live the rest of our lives.

In other words, Merton's peace was not cheap. This is not a cheap peace, or a cheap nonviolence, to paraphrase Bonhoeffer. Merton's peace was costly; it came at a great price, the consequence of his own cross, his own long-suffering for peace and disarmament. If we dare approach his spirit as he stood before the Buddhist statues of Polonnaruwa, we too must speak out against war and injustice, speak up for peace and nonviolence, and take public risks for God's reign of peace, no matter how many dismiss us or reject us, including family, friends, or church leaders. Living into the emptiness and compassion that Merton speaks of does not allow us to sit back and do nothing, or even to give up the struggle for justice and peace. This invitation into emptiness and compassion is for peacemakers, those who carry on the public struggle for justice and disarmament, those who accompany the nonviolent Jesus as he carries the cross of resistance to the culture of war. In other words, it is intended for every Christian.

Merton is not speaking about a comfortable spirituality where we just talk the talk. He also walked the walk, and wants us to do the same, and that walk is quite specific—it's the way of the cross, in the footsteps of the nonviolent Jesus in opposition to the culture of violence and war, come what may. It's not a middle-class life that turns its back on the suffering people of the world. If, like Merton, we pursue the vision of peace, nonviolence, and justice, and accompany the nonviolent Jesus into kenosis and compassion, we, too, will become, like Merton, Christian saints and Buddhist bodhisattvas.

Then, one day, like Merton our teacher, we will breathe in the risen Christ's spirit of peace and enter the new life of resurrection peace, in peaceful emptiness and perfect compassion for one and all.

Alleluia, Christ Is Risen

If Jesus really rose from the dead, then everything is up for grabs. That's the core message of the Gospels. He was perfectly nonviolent, taught loving nonviolence, resisted systemic injustice, and was summarily arrested, tortured, and executed for his peacemaking work. But lo and behold! The disciples announced that he rose from the dead. They said they saw him, in the flesh, and that he was just as gentle, loving, forgiving, and nonviolent as before, and because of that, they were going ahead to practice his same loving nonviolence. Everything now had changed.

Today I wonder who really believes in resurrection. For me, resurrection means having nothing to do with death. Resurrection means not having a trace of violence within us. We practice the loving nonviolence of the risen Jesus. We welcome his resurrection gift of peace, forgive everyone who ever hurt us, and go forth into the culture of violence and war announcing God's reign of nonviolence and peace.

One way to understand our calling as peacemakers is to see this life within the resurrection of the nonviolent Jesus. If "the way of the cross" means practicing steadfast nonviolent resistance to the culture of violence and war and peacefully accepting the consequences, living a resurrection life means renouncing fear and violence, living in the peace of the risen Jesus, and acting now as if the eternal life of peace has begun. Not only do we not own guns or serve the military or work for the nuclear industry, we live simply, stay in touch with the earth, serve the poor, and maintain a certain level of peace and compassion—no matter what happens to us. We know that our survival is guaranteed. We trust the God of peace. We believe that we will see our loved ones again, that all humanity is headed toward a new realm of love and peace, and that we will stand in heaven with the risen, nonviolent Jesus. We live now in intimate relationship with the risen, nonviolent Jesus, and that relationship changes the way we act in this world of violence and permanent war.

Who believes such unbelievable notions? Thomas Merton, for starters. He lived as if the resurrection of the nonviolent Jesus were true. He acted as if Jesus is not dead, knowing that Jesus is actually alive, right now, and that we are all headed toward resurrection. He took Jesus's Sermon on the Mount teachings seriously, practiced a strict regimen of prayer, gave his full attention to the God of peace, and told the world about Christ's reign of peace.

Merton, one could conclude, spent his life getting ready for resurrection. He knew that the resurrection of Jesus changes everything, including the way we relate to those around us, the church, and the world.

That's one of his greatest gifts, and greatest teachings for us. If we want to be peacemakers, we, too, need to believe in the risen Jesus, act as if resurrection were true, renounce every trace of violence and death, welcome the risen Jesus's gift of peace, and get ready for resurrection.

Because of the daily Trappist liturgical life, Merton was always chanting the resurrection word, "Alleluia." Through his deep reading, openhearted meditation, and profound faith, he knew that death comes to us all, but that death does not get the last word. He understood better than most that life is stronger than death, love is stronger than hate or fear, nonviolence is stronger than violence, peace is stronger than war. Merton's life was a long-suffering love, but it was also a long, peaceful preparation for resurrection. In many ways, "Alleluia!" was the theme of Merton's life.

Once, while Merton was introducing a friend of his to the abbot in his office, another monk interrupted with news that a beloved older monk had just died. "Alleluia!" Merton and the abbot said simultaneously. Merton's friend was stunned.

In 1975, an Easter sermon by Thomas Merton was published

as a small booklet titled *He Is Risen.* "Christ lives," Merton says at the start. "Christ is the Lord of the living and the dead. He is the Lord of history. He not only holds the beginning and the end in his hands, but he is in history with us, walking ahead of us to where we are going."[1] In his sermon, we catch a bit of Merton's passionate faith in the risen Christ and begin to understand the solid foundation for his monastic life and prophetic peace work. It's one of my favorite essays by Merton. He writes,

> We are called not only to believe that Christ once rose from the dead, thereby proving that he was God; we are called to experience the resurrection in our own lives by entering into this dynamic movement by following Christ who lives in us. This life, this dynamism, is expressed by the power of love and of encounter: Christ lives in us if we love one another. And our love for one another means involvement in one another's history. Christ lives in us and leads us into a new future which we build together for one another. That future is called the Kingdom of God. . . . We cooperate with him in bringing it to perfection. Such is the timeless message of the Church not only on Easter Sunday but every day of the year and every year until the world's end.[2]

From the start, the key for Merton is the word *experience.* We have all met the risen Christ in our lives, but like the downcast disciples on the road to Emmaus, few recognize him. But we act in faith for the risen Jesus, and so we practice his teachings of peace and love. The life of peace, love, and compassion is the way to make resurrection a daily experience, to let the risen Christ live in us. This is critically important for everyone who strives to be a Beatitude peacemaker. On the one hand, we do not work for the big business of death. We have nothing to do with war, killing, weapons, or the culture of war. On the other hand, we practice peace and nonviolence in our daily lives and support the grassroots movements of peace and nonviolence that are disarming the world. Peacemakers, in other words, are people of resurrection.

Merton continues,

A Christian bases his entire life on these truths. His entire
life is changed by the presence and the action of the risen
Christ. He knows he has encountered the risen Christ. . . .
True encounter with Christ in the word of God awakens
something in the depth of our being, something we did
not know was there. True encounter with Christ liberates
something in us, a power we did not know we had, a hope,
a capacity for life, a resilience, an ability to bounce back
when we thought we were completely defeated, a capacity
to grow and change, a power of creative transformation.[3]

Merton invites us to reflect on those moments in our lives when
we have encountered the risen Christ and to let the risen Christ
liberate us from violence and the culture of war. Those Upper
Room/Emmaus encounters should liberate us, give us hope, fill
us with new life, and help us to bounce back from defeat.

One key ingredient of the resurrection life, according to Merton, is "resiliency," "a capacity to grow and change," "a power
of creative transformation." As resurrection people, we bounce
back with new life, new faith, new hope, and new love, no matter
what happens in our personal lives or in the world. We know that
death does not get the last word, so we keep on going, walking
the path of peace and nonviolence, even if everyone around us
is consumed with violence and war. We keep practicing peace
and nonviolence. We go on, we continue to grow, we change,
we become better peacemakers.

The key to the resurrection life of peace is the fundamental
truth at the center of our faith lives: in the risen Jesus, death
does not get the last word. Therefore, no matter what happens,
our survival is guaranteed. We will dwell in the peace of Christ
for eternity, and that eternity has begun today. Merton writes,

For the Christian there is no defeat, because Christ is risen
and lives in us and Christ has overcome all that seeks to
destroy us or to block our human and spiritual growth....
How many Christians dare to believe that he who is risen
with Christ enjoys the liberty of the sons and daughters
of God and is not bound by the restrictions and taboos of
human prejudice? To be risen with Christ means not only

that one has a choice and that one may live by a higher law—the law of grace and love—but that one must do so.[4]

These Christian beliefs are central to peacemaking. Christ our risen peacemaker lives in us, so we go forth, without any fear, including the fear of death, and let Christ live in us. We carry on the work of Christ the peacemaker, and let the fruits of his resurrection blossom in our lives. We claim our true identities as sons and daughters of the God of peace; therefore, we practice the peace and nonviolence of the nonviolent Jesus who was executed but lives on. We become, like the nonviolent Jesus, crucified and risen peacemakers.

Thomas Merton was a rare, mature, believing Christian, like his peers Dorothy Day, Martin Luther King Jr., and Daniel Berrigan. He knew that a mature Christian walks the way of resurrection, and so lives in peace and nonviolence, but he also knew that every mature Christian must walk the way of the cross, must continue the peace work of Jesus by nonviolently resisting violence and the culture of war:

> The risen life is not easy; it is also a dying life. The presence of the resurrection in our lives means the presence of the cross, for we do not rise with Christ unless we also first die with him. It is by the cross that we enter the dynamism of creative transformation, the dynamism of resurrection and renewal, the dynamism of love.[5]

As people of the cross and resurrection, we follow the nonviolent Jesus. We are disciples and apostles, which means, in a world of permanent war and nuclear weapons, we are peacemakers, practitioners of gospel nonviolence. We go against the grain, rock the boat, upset the status quo, and agitate for justice and disarmament morning, noon, and night. This will get us into trouble, as it did Jesus, but then, it provides us with new opportunities to practice nonviolence, make peace, and witness on behalf of the risen Jesus. Merton continues,

> Jesus was condemned on the charge that he was a revolutionary, a subversive radical, fighting for the overthrow of

legitimate government. His death and resurrection were the culminating battle in his fight to liberate us from all forms of tyranny, all forms of domination by anything or anyone except the Spirit, the Law of Love, the "purpose and grace" of God.

The Christian must have the courage to follow Christ. The Christian who is risen in Christ must dare to be like Christ. He must dare to follow conscience even in unpopular causes. He must, if necessary, be able to disagree with the majority and make decisions that he knows to be according to the Gospel and the teaching of Christ, even when others do not understand why he is acting this way.

The Christian in whom Christ is risen dares to think and act differently from the crowd. He has ideas of his own, not because he is arrogant, but because he has humility to stand alone and pay attention to the purpose and the grace of God, which are often quite contrary to the purposes and the plans of an established human power structure.

If we have risen with Christ then we must dare to stand by him in the loneliness of his passion, when the entire establishment both religious and civil turned against him as a modern state would turn against a dangerous radical.[6]

These passages are the key to understanding Merton's Christian life and work for peace. We go forward in our work for peace and justice, first of all, because Jesus is risen and alive. He practiced peace and nonviolence, so we do the same. We have risen with Christ, therefore we carry on Christ's work and speak out against war and injustice with him, come what may.

Merton warns us "not to be afraid to be a Christian." The nonviolent Jesus is the only one worth following, he suggests, so let's place our bet with him, and go forward with full confidence in his resurrection, and carry on his work for justice and peace.

[Some Christians are] not content with faith in the risen Christ, not content with the grace and love of Christ: they want the comfort and justification of being on the side of wealth and power. In some cases, Christianity becomes literally the religion of overkill: the religion in which you prove your fidelity to Christ by your willingness to destroy his enemies ten times over. In order to do this you have to conveniently forget all those disturbing statements in the New Testament about the love of enemies!

Though we may still "say" with our lips that Christ is risen, we secretly believe him, in practice, to be dead. And we believe that there is a massive stone blocking the way and keeping us from getting to his dead body. Our Christian religion too often becomes simply the cult of the dead body of Christ compounded with anguish and desperation over the problem of moving the immovable stone that keeps us from reaching him. This is no joke. This is what actually happens to the Christian religion when it ceases to be a reality living faith and becomes a mere legalistic and ritualistic formality.

Such Christianity is no longer life in the risen Christ but a formula cult of the dead Christ considered not as the Light and Savior of the world but as a kind of divine "thing," an extremely holy object, a theological relic. This is the result of substituting something else for the Living Presence and Light of Christ in our lives. Instead of the unspeakable, invisible, yet terribly near and powerful presence of the Living Lord, we set up a structure of pious images and abstract concepts until Christ becomes a shadow.[7]

"We must never let our religious ideas, customs, rituals, and conventions become more real to us than the risen Christ."[8] Merton urges us to believe with all our hearts in the resurrection of Jesus, and its social, economic, and political implications of our lives. He wants us to take the resurrection seriously. We do that by basing our lives and acting daily according to the life and teachings of the nonviolent Jesus. We become passionate people of universal love, active nonviolence, and boundless compassion. Like Merton, we become authentic peacemakers to the world of violence and war, and let the chips fall where they may.

"Jesus is not dead," Merton announces in his Easter sermon. "He is not an inert object, not a lifeless thing, not a piece of property, not a super-religious heirloom. He is risen. . . . He is going before us into his Kingdom! Alleluia!"[9]

We can choose to follow the risen Christ into his Kingdom of peace and nonviolence just as Merton did. We, too, can go through life chanting "Alleluia," if we want. This, Merton insists, is the way of the Christian. We are people of the resurrection, and so we live and witness to the peace of the risen Christ.

In the end, that's the lesson of Thomas Merton's life—and the key to our own peacemaking lives.

27

In the Midst of Death,
the Celebration of Life

Despite the seriousness of Merton's monastic life and apocalyptic warnings to address the crises of violence that plague us, Merton calls us to celebrate the fullness of life, love, and peace.

Life is a great gift. We get to live and love and enjoy peace. Instead of death, we can choose, like Merton, to live life to the full. Life is too short to bother any longer with the big business of death and its petty metaphors. We do our best to speak out and resist the culture of war and death, but no matter what, we try to live life to the full, even unto our last breath. With Merton, we remember that we are created for love—created to love ourselves, love one another, love all creatures, all creation, and our loving Creator. So we go forward, in love and hope, curious about life, living life, not living death. We are at peace. Every step for the rest of our lives brings peace.

The fullness of life, the fullness of love, the fullness of peace—this is the milieu of the peacemaker. In the end, this is what Thomas Merton invites us to celebrate with gusto. He knows well that if we are going to spend our lives as peacemakers resisting death and the forces of death, we better live life to the full.

In a famous passage in *The Sign of Jonas*, Merton described being swept up one day in waves of consolation, peace, and joy. I believe the God of peace wants us all to live in such consolation, even as we try our best to work for justice and disarmament, to abolish war and injustice. Here's Merton's journal entry:

Love sails me around the house. I walk two steps on the ground and four steps in the air. It is love. It is consolation. I don't care if it is consolation. I am not attached to consolation. I love God. Love carries me all around. I don't want to do anything but love. And when the bell rings it is like pulling teeth to make myself shift because of that love, secret love, hidden love, obscure love, down inside me and outside me where I don't care to talk about it. I have only time for eternity, which is to say for love, love, love. Love is pushing me around the monastery, love is kicking me all around like a gong I tell you, love is the only thing that makes it possible for me to continue to tick. . . . Love is the door to eternity and the one who loves God is playing on the doorstep of eternity and before anything can happen love will have drawn him over the sill and closed the door and he won't bother about the world burning because he will know nothing but love.[1]

I love this passage. When things get too heavy for me, I remember it, read it, slow down, take heart, and try to recapture that spirit of consoling love, peace, and joy. I, too, want to spend my days in love, love, love. I don't want to go through life having done everything well—including witness to the gospel of Christ—without having loved myself, and others, and God. Love is the whole point, the reason for existence, the nature of God, our ultimate calling, our final end. Love is the means and the ends for the peacemaker. More, love reminds us that we are just instruments of God's peace. God does the peacemaking. The outcome is in God's hands, not ours. We are no longer attached to the results of all our efforts for justice and peace. We give our lives for justice and peace, but most of all, we love everyone and celebrate life. Our focus remains on the God of peace and love.

Throughout his writings, essays, and letters, Merton summons us to the fullness of life, love, and peace. In the conclusion of *New Seeds of Contemplation*, he writes beautifully about God at play among humanity in the wonders of creation. This, Merton insists, should be the center of our lives; we, too, are at play with God in creation. This is the fruit of contemplative peace and nonviolence—to discover God in the beauty of creation and its creatures, in the laughter of children, in the love for sisters and brothers. This vision of God at play among us, in creation, is the motivation behind our work for peace and justice. We simply try to help others enter God's reign of peace and nonviolence so that more and more people will renounce the big business of death and live life to the full. Here's Merton, writing in full mode, about the fullness of life with God:

> What is serious to people is often very trivial in the sight of God. What in God might appear to us as "play" is perhaps what God himself takes most seriously. The Lord plays and diverts Himself in the garden of his creation, and if we could let go of our own obsession with what we think is the meaning of it all, we might be able to hear God's call and follow God in his mysterious, cosmic dance. We do not have to go very far to catch echoes of that game, and of that dancing.
>
> When we are alone on a starlit night; when by chance we see the migrating birds in autumn descending on a grove of junipers to rest and eat; when we see children in a moment when they are really children; when we know love in our own hearts; or when, like the Japanese poet Basho we hear an old frog land in a quiet pond with a solitary splash—at such times the awakening, the turning inside out of all values, the "newness," the emptiness and the purity of vision that make themselves evident, provide a glimpse of the cosmic dance.
>
> For the world and time are the dance of the Lord in emptiness. The silence of the spheres is the music of a wedding feast. The more we persist in misunderstanding the phenomena of life, the more we analyze them out into strange finalities and complex purposes of our own, the more we involve ourselves in sadness, absurdity and despair. But it does not matter much, because no despair of ours can alter the reality of things, or stain the joy of the cosmic dance. Which is always there. Indeed, we are in the midst of it, and it is in the midst of us, for it beats in our very blood, whether we want it to or not. We are invited

to forget ourselves on purpose, cast our awful solemnity
to the winds, and join in the general dance.[2]

Join the cosmic dance! What a beautiful invitation! Peacemakers spend their days noncooperating with the culture of war and
death. They practice nonviolence, make peace, love everyone
unconditionally, speak out publicly on the hardest issues, advocate for God's reign of justice and peace, teach the Sermon on
the Mount, take risks for disarmament, and uphold the vision of
a new culture of peace and nonviolence. None of this is easy. It
brings disruption, rejection, persecution, harassment, and worse.
But as followers of the nonviolent Jesus, we walk the path of
peace, the way of the cross, and at the same time, the way of
resurrection, so we celebrate the slight edge of life over death, and
live life to the full. We join the cosmic dance as God celebrates
life with creation and God's beloved sons and daughters.

To celebrate life as Merton did means enjoying the present
moment of peace, taking time every day to dwell in the beauty
of creation, loving those around us, encouraging one and all,
bringing peace and joy to others, showing kindness to everyone,
serving the marginalized and disenfranchised, and giving thanks
and praise at all times. We celebrate all God's creatures—every
sister and brother, every bird, fish, and animal. We celebrate
births and weddings and children and older people and the stars
and the rain and sunrises and sunsets and the desert and the
ocean. We recognize every human being as a sister and brother;
there are no more enemies, everyone is our friend. Even in the
midst of suffering and death, we dwell in peace, with our hearts
centered in the ongoing, permanent wedding banquet of life,
knowing that one day everyone will be healed and celebrate
with joy in the presence of the God of peace.

This is what Thomas Merton, monk, hermit, and peacemaker,
reminds us. He kept going forward, resilient to the end, taking
off to explore New Mexico, California, Alaska, India, Sri Lanka,
and Thailand, filled with life, eager to love, pointing everyone
back to the God of peace. He was a pilgrim of peace who resisted
the culture of death, danced in the water of life, loved the God
of peace, and offered God's peace to one and all.

That may be his greatest gift and lesson—that we, too, might fulfill our vocations to be peacemakers, God's sons and daughters, who resist the forces of death, live life to the full, serve the God of peace, and join the cosmic dance with the God of peace amid the beauty of creation.

As we do, we receive Christ's resurrection gift of peace and realize that we have already arrived home. We have entered the eternal present moment of peace in the presence of the God of peace. "That is to say, the wind blows through the trees, and you breathe it."

We have become who we were created to be. Eternal peace, love, and joy have begun. We are there. We are all one.

We are, finally, at peace.

Conclusion

"Blessed are the peacemakers," Jesus announced in the Sermon on the Mount. "They shall be called the sons and daughters of the God of peace."

Thomas Merton lived as if he were the beloved son of the God of peace. Through a lifetime of contemplative prayer, monastic silence, daily mindfulness, scripture study, community sharing, wilderness living, and prophetic writing, he claimed his core fundamental identity as the beloved son of the God of peace and acted as if this identity were true and thus fulfilled his vocation to be a peacemaker.

Each one of us is likewise called to claim our core identity as a son or daughter of the God of peace, and to fulfill our vocation to be peacemaker.

Thomas Merton wrote over a hundred books, thousands of letters, and countless other unpublished material. There is so much more to be said about Merton. We will reflect on the gift of his life and wisdom for many years to come. As I ponder the cumulative impact of his life one hundred years after his birth, I find three simple lessons on peace that challenge us to carry on the journey of peace. I'd like to conclude with these lessons and invitations as we carry on our own journey to peace.

Claim Your True Self as the Beloved Son or Daughter of the God of Peace

Thomas Merton invites us to claim our core fundamental identities beyond the narrow confines of culture and nation as the beloved sons and daughters of the God of peace, and therefore the brothers and sisters of every human being. That means that we, too, take time each day in contemplative prayer, mindfulness, silence, solitude, and scripture study, to discover our true selves, claim our identities as sons and daughters of the God of peace, and make that truth true in our daily lives.

This is the one necessary thing, as the Gospels put it, and it is doable. As contemplative peacemakers in the tradition of Thomas Merton, we can sit in silence and peace every day for thirty to sixty minutes, notice our breath, breathe in the Holy Spirit of peace and love, and enter into the presence of the God of peace. As the Gospels teach, the God of peace loves each one of us infinitely, unconditionally, and personally, and calls us, "My beloved."

God loves you, and it's good to take time from our busy day to sit and let the God of peace love us, to be God's beloved son or daughter. If we do this regularly, daily, faithfully, we will live our way into its truth and find ourselves disarmed, healed, and more and more peaceful. We will also begin to see the world with new eyes, through the eyes of peace and nonviolence. Because we are sons and daughters of the God of peace and universal love, we will begin to practice peace and universal love. We will become people of contemplative, active, and prophetic nonviolence all at once, just like Thomas Merton.

Live Every Day in Peace with the God of Peace, All Humanity, and All Creation

Over time, as we realize who we are and claim our funda-mental nature and identity every day as the beloved son or daughter of the God of peace, we will begin to live and act, as Thomas Merton did, in intimate relationship with the God of peace, as citizens of God's kingdom of peace and nonviolence, here and now, and from now on. Our lives will be rooted and based in this intimate relationship with the God of peace, with the nonviolent Jesus and with the Holy Spirit of peace. Our lives and journeys will flow from this source of peace and nonviolent love in the God of peace. We see our lives in relationship and discipleship to the nonviolent Jesus, as Merton did, and so we walk with Jesus on the journey of peace, love, and nonviolence, even to our own crosses into the new life of resurrection peace.

Like Merton, we find ourselves at one with God, with humanity and with all creation. We live with Wisdom, our peacemaking, feminine God. We see every human being as a sister and brother, shining like the sun, already children of the God of peace, even if they do not know it. We live at home in the universe, at one with creation, and enjoy the beauty of all God's creatures and creation itself. In our meekness, our nonviolence, we inherit the earth, as the Beatitudes promise.

Because we live in relationship with the God of peace, we are being disarmed and practice nonviolence. We renounce violence, get rid of our guns, quit the military, refuse to support war or weapons, and learn the wisdom of nonviolence as active love pursuing the truth of our common unity, even to the point where we give our lives nonviolently for our sisters and brothers, for creation itself, as Jesus did.

As people of faith and prayer, we engage in contemplative nonviolence and live a new spirituality of peace and nonviolence. We know with Merton that nonviolence depends entirely on God and God's word, so we rely solely on the God of peace, not on the false gods of war and weapons. Like Merton, we make our entire lives a rejection of war, violence, nuclear weapons, corporate greed, systemic injustice, empire, and environmental destruction. We live out Merton's prayer of union with the God of peace and universal communion with every human being, all creatures, and all creation.

We live in peace with ourselves, all people, and all creation. We practice nonviolence toward ourselves, all people, and all creation. Along the way, we discover, like Merton, that we are already one, and that wisdom becomes our secret joy and our inner motivation.

Go Forth into the World of War as a Peacemaker

As we claim our true identities as sons and daughters of the God of peace and live the rest of our lives like Merton in intimate relationship with the God of peace and the nonviolent Jesus, we then go forth publicly as peacemakers into the world of war and violence. We practice gospel nonviolence and teach peace. We live in solidarity with the poor, with those declared to be our nation's enemy, and with all creation. We learn the methodology of nonviolence, nonviolent resistance to systemic evil, and nonviolent conflict resolution. We support the global grassroots movements of nonviolence around the world. We undertake peacemaking as "a work of hope," and join the nonviolent struggle to abolish war, systemic injustice, nuclear weapons, poverty, corporate greed, hunger, racism, sexism, and environmental destruction. In other words, we at once announce and welcome God's reign of peace, love, and nonviolence here on earth. So we are not afraid to speak out boldly, publicly, and prophetically for justice and disarmament.

For us, like Merton, everything is emptiness, everything is compassion. We live now in the resurrection peace of the risen Christ, so like Merton, our lives have become one long "Alleluia!" We, too, celebrate life and live life to the full, even as we publicly, nonviolently resist the forces and structures of death. We have become peacemakers and spend the rest of our days making peace, teaching peace, spreading peace, and being the peace we seek.

This is our highest calling. Thomas Merton, our teacher and guide, gives us the example of his life to inspire us to fulfill our own calling to be peacemakers, the beloved sons and daughters of the God of peace.

The world does not need any more warmakers. Nor does the church. We need more peacemakers. We need nonviolent Christians who follow the peacemaking Christ. Thomas Merton calls us to discover our true selves and fulfill our own particular mission as peacemakers who follow the peacemaking Christ and announce the coming of a new nonviolent world of peace.

Each one of us can do this. Each one of us can be a peacemaker. Each one of us can bring our own unique contribution to the way of peace and nonviolence, inspire others to live nonviolently and help disarm the world. With Thomas Merton as our teacher, friend and guide, we go forth renewed to proclaim peace to the world, and show everyone what it looks like through our own peacemaking lives.

With Thomas Merton, may we fulfill our calling to be peacemakers, and spend our days giving glory to the God of peace through Gospel nonviolence.

About the Author

"John Dear is the embodiment of a peacemaker," Archbishop Desmond Tutu wrote a few years ago when he nominated John for the Nobel Peace Prize. "He has led by example through his actions and in his writings and in numerous sermons, speeches, and demonstrations. He believes that peace is not something static, but rather to make peace is to be engaged, mind, body, and spirit. His teaching is to love yourself, to love your neighbor, your enemy, and to love the world and to understand the profound responsibility in doing all of these. He is a man who has the courage of his convictions and who speaks out and acts against war, the manufacture of weapons, and any situation where a human being might be at risk through violence. For evil to prevail requires only that good people sit on the sidelines and do nothing. John Dear is compelling all of us to stand up and take responsibility for the suffering of humanity so often caused through selfishness and greed."

John Dear has spent over three decades speaking to people around the world about the gospel of Jesus, the way of nonviolence, and the call to make peace. A Catholic priest, he has served as the director of the Fellowship of Reconciliation, the largest interfaith peace organization in the United States, and after September 11, 2001, as one of the Red Cross coordinators of chaplains at the Family Assistance Center, counseling thousands of relatives and rescue workers. He has worked in homeless shelters, soup kitchens, and community centers; traveled in war zones around the world, including Iraq, Palestine, Nicaragua, Afghanistan, and Colombia; lived in El Salvador, Guatemala, and Northern Ireland; been arrested over seventy-five times in acts of civil disobedience against war; and spent eight months in prison for a Plowshares disarmament action. In the 1990s he arranged for Mother Teresa to speak to various governors to stop the death penalty. He has two master's degrees in theology from the Graduate Theological Union in California, and has taught theology at Fordham University.

John Dear has been featured in the *New York Times*, the *Washington Post*, *USA Today*, National Public Radio's *All Things Considered*, and elsewhere. For many years, he wrote a weekly blog for the *National Catholic Reporter*, and is featured regularly on the national radio show *Democracy Now!* and the Huffington Post. He is the subject of the DVD documentary *The Narrow Path* (with music by Joan Baez and Jackson Browne) and is profiled in *John Dear on Peace*, by Patti Normile (St. Anthony Messenger Press, 2009). His nearly thirty books, including *Living Peace, The Nonviolent Life, Lazarus Come Forth, The God of Peace, Jesus the Rebel, Disarming the Heart*, and his autobiography *A Persistent Peace*, have been translated into ten languages. John Dear is on the staff of Pace e Bene and www. campaignnonviolence.org. He lives in northern New Mexico.

For further information, see www.johndear.org.

Notes

Chapter 1

[1]Thomas Merton, unpublished essay, "The Monastery of Christ in the Desert."
[2]Ibid.
[3]Thomas Merton, *Woods, Shore, Desert* (Santa Fe: Museum of New Mexico Press, 1982), 48.

Chapter 4

[1]Thomas Merton, *Gandhi on Nonviolence* (New York: New Directions, 1964), 6.
[2]Ibid., 43.
[3]Ibid., 23.

Chapter 5

[1]Thomas Merton, "Blessed Are the Meek," in Christine Bochen, ed., *Thomas Merton: Essential Writings* (Maryknoll, NY: Orbis Books, 2000), 134.

Chapter 6

[1]Thomas Merton, *The Hidden Ground of Love: Letters, Volume 1*, ed. William Shannon (New York: Farrar, Straus, and Giroux, 1985), 349.
[2]Ibid., 140.
[3]Jim Forest, *Living with Wisdom: A Life of Thomas Merton* (Maryknoll, NY: Orbis Books, 2008), 153–54; Thomas Merton, "The Root of War Is Fear," *Catholic Worker*, October 1961.

Chapter 7

[1]Jim Forest, *Living with Wisdom: A Life of Thomas Merton* (Maryknoll, NY: Orbis Books, 2008), 165–66; Thomas Merton, *Honorable Reader*, ed. Robert Daggy (New York: Crossroad, 1989), 63–67.

[2]Quoted in Forest, *Living with Wisdom*, 159.

[3]Quoted in ibid., 216; Thomas Merton, *Faith and Violence* (Notre Dame, IN: Notre Dame Press, 1968).

Chapter 8

[1]Thomas Merton, *Conjectures of a Guilty Bystander* (New York: Doubleday, 1965), 140–42; see also Jim Forest, *Living with Wisdom: A Life of Thomas Merton* (Maryknoll, NY: Orbis Books, 2008), 133–34. For the complete original, see Thomas Merton, *A Search for Solitude: Journals, Three*, ed. Lawrence Cunningham (San Francisco: HarperSanFrancisco, 1996), 181–82.

Chapter 9

[1]Thomas Merton, *Turning toward the World: Journals, Four*, ed. Victor Kramer (San Francisco: HarperSanFrancisco, 1996), 238–39.

[2]Thomas Merton, "Blessed Are the Meek," in *Thomas Merton: Essential Writings*, ed. Christine Bochen (Maryknoll, NY: Orbis Books, 2000), 123.

[3]Ibid., 124–25.

[4]Ibid., 126.

[5]Thomas Merton, *A Vow of Conversation*, ed. Naomi Burton Stone (New York: Farrar, Straus, and Giroux, 1988), 31–32.

[6]Thomas Merton, *Seeds of Destruction* (New York: Farrar, Straus, and Giroux, 1964), 128–30.

[7]See Merton, "Blessed Are the Meek," 129–34.

[8]Thomas Merton, "Blessed Are the Meek," in *The Nonviolent Alternative*, ed. Gordan Zahn (New York: Farrar, Straus, and Giroux, 1980), 217.

[9]Thomas Merton, "Peace and Revolution," in *The Nonviolent Alternative*, 75.

Chapter 10

[1]Thomas Merton, *Entering the Silence: Journals, Two*, ed. Jonathan Montaldo (San Francisco: HarperSanFrancisco, 1996), 398–99.

[2]Thomas Merton, *Dancing in the Water of Life: Journals, Five*, ed. Robert Daggy (San Francisco: HarperSanFrancisco, 1997), 200.

[3]Ibid., 195.

[4]Ibid., 253–54.

[5]Ibid., 264–65.

[6]Thomas Merton, *A Search for Solitude: Journals, Three*, ed. Lawrence Cunningham (San Francisco: HarperSanFrancisco, 1996), 28–29.

Chapter 11

[1]Thomas Merton, *A Vow of Conversation*, ed. Naomi Burton Stone (New York: Farrar, Straus, and Giroux, 1988), 152.

²Ibid., 206.
³Ibid., 103.
⁴Ibid., 174.
⁵Ibid., 142.
⁶Ibid., 188.
⁷Ibid., 204.

Chapter 12

¹Thomas Merton, "Day of a Stranger," in *A Thomas Merton Reader*, ed. Thomas McDonnell (New York: Doubleday, 1974), 433; see also the original in Thomas Merton, *Dancing in the Water of Life, Journals, Five*, ed. Robert Daggy (San Francisco: HarperSanFrancisco, 1997), 239ff.
²Merton, *Thomas Merton Reader*, 432–33.
³Ibid., 431.
⁴Thomas Merton, *A Vow of Conversation*, ed. Naomi Burton Stone (New York: Farrar, Straus, and Giroux, 1988), 127.
⁵Ibid., 128.
⁶Merton, *Thomas Merton Reader*, 127.

Chapter 13

¹Thomas Merton, "Peace and Revolution," in *The Nonviolent Alternative*, ed. Gordon Zahn (New York: Farrar, Straus, and Giroux, 1980), 259.
²Ibid.
³Ibid.
⁴Gordon Oyer, *Pursuing the Spiritual Roots of Protest* (Eugene, OR: Cascade Books, 2014).

Chapter 14

¹Thomas Merton, "Peace and Protest," in *The Nonviolent Alternative*, ed. Gordon Zahn (New York: Farrar, Straus, and Giroux, 1980), 67–68.
²Ibid., 68–69.
³Thomas Merton, *The Hidden Ground of Love: Letters, Volume 1*, ed. William Shannon (New York: Farrar, Straus, and Giroux, 1985), 294–97.
⁴Robert Gaggen, ed., *Striving towards Being: The Letters of Thomas Merton and Czeslaw Milosz* (New York: Farrar, Straus, and Giroux, 1997), 52.
⁵Ibid., 19–20.

Chapter 15

¹Thomas Merton, *The Nonviolent Alternative*, ed. Gordon Zahn (New York: Farrar, Straus, and Giroux, 1980), 263–64.
²Ibid., 264.

Chapter 16

[1]Patrick Hart, ed., *Survival or Prophecy: The Letters of Thomas Merton and Jean Leclercq* (New York: Farrar, Straus, and Giroux, 2002), 175.

Chapter 17

[1]Thomas Merton, *The Road to Joy: Letters*, ed. Robert Daggy (New York: Farrar, Straus, and Giroux, 1989), 41–42.

[2]Thomas Merton, *Conjectures of a Guilty Bystander* (New York: Doubleday, 1965), 251.

[3]Thomas Merton, *Turning toward the World: Journals, Four*, ed. Victor Kramer (San Francisco: HarperSanFrancisco, 1996), 174.

[4]Ibid., 182.

[5]Ibid., 238–39.

[6]Thomas Merton, *The Hidden Ground of Love: Letters, Volume 1*, ed. William Shannon (New York: Farrar, Straus, and Giroux, 1985), 70–71.

[7]Ibid., 83–84.

[8]Ibid., 86.

[9]Ibid., 78.

[10]Ibid., 81.

[11]Ibid., 90.

[12]Ibid., 92.

[13]Ibid., 98.

Chapter 18

[1]Thomas Merton, *The Seven Storey Mountain* (New York: Harcourt Brace, 1948), 237–38.

[2]S. T. Georgiou, *The Way of the Dreamcatcher: Spirit Lessons with Robert Lax: Poet, Peacemaker, Sage* (n.p.: Novalis, 2002), 68.

[3]Ibid.

Chapter 19

[1]Thomas Merton, *The Nonviolent Alternative*, ed. Gordon Zahn (New York: Farrar, Straus, and Giroux, 1980), 260.

[2]Ibid., 261.

[3]Ibid.

[4]Ibid., 165–66.

[5]Ibid.

[6]Ibid., 167.

[7]Ibid., 138.

Chapter 20

[1]Thomas Merton, *The Nonviolent Alternative*, ed. Gordon Zahn (New York: Farrar, Straus, and Giroux, 1980), 188.
[2]Ibid.
[3]Ibid., 160–61.
[4]Ibid., 161–62.

Chapter 21

[1]Thomas Merton, *The Nonviolent Alternative*, ed. Gordon Zahn (New York: Farrar, Straus, and Giroux, 1980), 3.
[2]Ibid., 6.
[3]Ibid., 9.
[4]Ibid., 10.
[5]Ibid.
[6]Ibid., 11.

Chapter 22

[1]Christopher Pramuk, *Sophia: The Hidden Christ of Thomas Merton* (Collegeville, MN: Liturgical Press, 2009), 194.
[2]Ibid., 281.
[3]Ibid., 281, xxiv.
[4]Thomas Merton, *A Thomas Merton Reader*, ed. Thomas McDonnell (New York: Doubleday, 1974), 506.
[5]Jim Forest, *Living with Wisdom: A Life of Thomas Merton* (Maryknoll, NY: Orbis Books, 2008), 147.
[6]Merton, *Thomas Merton Reader*, 507.
[7]Ibid., 508.
[8]Ibid., 509.
[9]Ibid., 510.
[10]Pramuk, *Sophia*, 74.
[11]Ibid., xix.
[12]Ibid., xxiii.
[13]Ibid., 124.
[14]Merton, *Thomas Merton Reader*, 506–8; Pramuk, *Sophia*, 97.
[15]Pramuk, *Sophia*, xxvi.
[16]Ibid., xxvi.
[17]Ibid., 128.
[18]Ibid., 132.
[19]Ibid., xxviii.
[20]Ibid., 296.

[21]Ibid., 296–97.
[22]Ibid., 173, 196.
[23]Merton, *Thomas Merton Reader*, 510.
[24]Pramuk, *Sophia*, 29.

Chapter 23

[1]John Howard Griffin, *A Hidden Wholeness* (Boston: Houghton Mifflin, 1979), 2–3.
[2]Thomas Merton, *Raids on the Unspeakable* (New York: New Directions, 1966), 9–10.
[3]Thomas Merton, *A Vow of Conversation*, ed. Naomi Burton Stone (New York: Farrar, Straus, and Giroux, 1988), 156.
[4]Thomas Merton, *Turning toward the World: Journals, Four*, ed. Victor Kramer (San Francisco: HarperSanFrancisco, 1996), 312.
[5]Merton, *Vow of Conversation*, 43–44.
[6]Thomas Merton, *Conjectures of a Guilty Bystander* (New York: Doubleday, 1965), 177–79.
[7]Thomas Merton, *New Seeds of Contemplation* (New York: New Directions, 1961), 30–32.
[8]Thomas Merton, *A Search for Solitude: Journals, Three*, ed. Lawrence Cunningham (San Francisco: HarperSanFrancisco, 1996), 29.

Chapter 24

[1]Thomas Merton, *A Thomas Merton Reader*, ed. Thomas McDonnell (New York: Doubleday, 1974), 447.
[2]Thomas Merton, *The Hidden Ground of Love: Letters, Volume 1*, ed. William Shannon (New York: Farrar, Straus, and Giroux, 1985), 63–64.
[3]Thomas Merton, *Seeds of Destruction* (New York: Farrar, Straus, and Giroux, 1980).
[4]Thomas Merton, *Conjectures of a Guilty Bystander* (New York: Doubleday, 1965), 12; Jim Forest, *Living with Wisdom: A Life of Thomas Merton* (Maryknoll, NY: Orbis Books, 2008), 129.
[5]Thomas Merton, *The Asian Journal of Thomas Merton* (New York: New Directions, 1973), 309.
[6]Ibid., 309–10.
[7]Ibid., 315–16.
[8]Ibid., 317.
[9]Ibid., 308–9.
[10]Ibid., 318–19.

Chapter 25

[1]Thomas Merton, *A Search for Solitude: Journals, Three*, ed. Lawrence Cunningham (San Francisco: HarperSanFrancisco, 1996), 39.

[2]Thomas Merton, *The Hidden Ground of Love: Letters, Volume 1*, ed. William Shannon (New York: Farrar, Straus, and Giroux, 1985), 52.

[3]Thomas Merton, *The Asian Journal of Thomas Merton* (New York: New Directions, 1973), 233–36; Merton, *The Other Side of the Mountain, Journals, Seven*, ed. Patrick Hart (San Francisco: HarperSanFrancisco, 1998), 323.

[4]James Douglass, *Lightning East to West* (New York: Crossroad, 1984), 95.

[5]Ibid., 95–96.

[6]The Dalai Lama, "Many Faiths, One Truth," *The New York Times*, May 24, 2012.

Chapter 26

[1]Christine Bochen, ed., *Thomas Merton: Essential Writings* (Maryknoll, NY: Orbis Books, 2000), 188; Thomas Merton, *He Is Risen* (Niles, IL: Argus, 1975), 5.

[2]Merton, *He Is Risen*, 8–10.

[3]Ibid., 12–15.

[4]Ibid., 16, 20–21.

[5]Ibid., 18.

[6]Ibid., 30, 22, 26–28.

[7]Ibid., 38–39, 48–51.

[8]Ibid., 52.

[9]Ibid., 57.

Chapter 27

[1]Thomas Merton, *A Thomas Merton Reader*, ed. Thomas McDonnell (New York: Doubleday, 1974), 190–91.

[2]Ibid., 504–5; Merton, *New Seeds of Contemplation* (New York: New Directions, 1961), 296–97.

Acknowledgements

Excerpts from *The Hidden Ground of Love: The Letters of Thomas Merton on Religious Experience and Social Concerns* by Thomas Merton, edited by William H. Shannon. Copyright © 1985 by the Merton Legacy Trust. Excerpts from *A Vow of Conversation: Journals 1964-1965* by Thomas Merton. Copyright © 1988 by the Merton Legacy Trust. Reprinted by permission of Farrar, Straus and Giroux, LLC.

Excerpts from *Seeds of Destruction* by Thomas Merton. Copyright © 1964 by The Abbey of Gethsemani. Copyright renewal 1992 by Robert Giroux, James Laughlin, and Tommy O'Callaghan. Reprinted by permission of Farrar, Straus and Giroux, LLC and Curtis Brown, Ltd.

Excerpts from *Faith and Violence* by Thomas Merton. Copyright © 1968 by the University of Notre Dame Press. Reprinted by permission of the University of Notre Dame Press.

Excerpts from *He is Risen* by Thomas Merton. Copyright © 1975 by Argus Communications. Reprinted by permission of the Merton Legacy Trust.

Excerpts from *The Way of the Dreamcatcher: Spirit Lessons with Robert Lax: Poet, Peacemaker*, Sage by S.T. Georgiou. Copyright © 2002 by S.T. Georgiou. Published in 2002 by Novalis and in 2010 by Templegate. Reprinted by permission of S.T. Georgiou.

Excerpts from *Conjectures of a Guilty Bystander* by Thomas Merton. Copyright © 1965, 1966 by The Abbey of Gethsemani. Used by permission of Doubleday, an imprint of the Knopf Doubleday Publishing Group, a division of Random House LLC. All rights reserved.

Excerpt from *Turning Toward the World: The Journals of Thomas Merton, Volume Four 1960-1963* by Thomas Merton and edited by Victor A. Kramer. Copyright © 1996 by The Merton Legacy Trust. Reprinted by permission of HarperCollins Publishers.

Excerpts from: *Emblems of a Season of Fury*, copyright ©1963 by The Abbey of Gethsemani, Inc.; from *New Seeds of Contemplation*, copyright ©1961 by The Abbey of Gethsemani, Inc.; from *Raids on the Unspeakable*, copyright ©1966 by The Abbey of Gethsemani, Inc.; from *The Asian Journals of Thomas Merton*, copyright ©1975 by The Trustees of the Merton Legacy Trust; "Original Child Bomb" from *The Collected Poems of Thomas Merton*, copyright ©1962 by The Abbey of Gethsemani, Inc.; "Chant To Be Used in Processions Around a Site With Furnaces" from *The Collected Poems of Thomas Merton*, copyright ©1963 by The Abbey of Gethsemani, Inc., 1977 by The Trustees of the Merton Legacy Trust. Reprinted by permission of New Directions Publishing Corp.